WOMEN & MONEY

WOMEN
& MONEY

SUZE
ORMAN

SPIEGEL & GRAU
NEW YORK

Published in the United States by Spiegel & Grau,
an imprint of Random House, a division of
Penguin Random House LLC, New York.

SPIEGEL & GRAU and colophon is a registered trademark
of Penguin Random House LLC.

Originally published in hardcover in different form in the United States
by Spiegel & Grau, an imprint of Random House,
a division of Penguin Random House LLC, in 2007,
and subsequently as a mass market paperback by Spiegel & Grau,
an imprint of Random House, a division of
Penguin Random House LLC, in 2010.

LIBRARY OF CONGRESS CATALOGING-IN-PUBLICATION DATA
Names: Orman, Suze, author.
Title: Women & money / Suze Orman.
Other titles: Women and money
Description: Revised Edition. | New York: Spiegel & Grau, 2018. | Revised
edition of the author's Women & money, c2007. | Includes index.
Identifiers: LCCN 2018019618 | ISBN 9780812987614 (hardback) |
ISBN 9780812987621 (ebook)
Subjects: LCSH: Women—United States—Finance, Personal. | Finance,
Personal—United States. | Wealth—Psychological aspects. | BISAC:
BUSINESS & ECONOMICS / Personal Finance / General. | BUSINESS &
ECONOMICS / Motivational. | SELF-HELP / Personal Growth / Success.
Classification: LCC HG181 .O75 2018 | DDC 332.0240082/0973—dc23
LC record available at https://lccn.loc.gov/2018019618

Printed in the United States of America on acid-free paper

spiegelandgrau.com
randomhousebooks.com

2 4 6 8 9 7 5 3 1

Revised Edition

To Esther Margolis

Who had the courage to publish my first book and the faith to send me, an unknown author, on a twenty-seven-city tour to promote it; who literally stood by my side when I was scared and stayed until I no longer felt afraid.

Dear Esther, I can't adequately express the immense gratitude I have for you. You started me on an extraordinary journey that has connected me with millions of people, all around the world. It is said that behind every great woman there stands an even greater woman, and, Esther, for me you are that woman.

CONTENTS

INTRODUCTION

When this book was first published in 2007, I was convinced that women were finally ready to focus on being powerful with their money. Indeed, many women heard the call. The book connected with a few million readers. It reached the top of the *New York Times* bestseller list, and tens of thousands of women took the lessons of the book to heart and forged healthy and strong relationships with their money.

But, in the years since, I've come to realize that many more women—even some who bought the book—continued to ignore their issues with money. Or they struggled to make confident decisions that would help them achieve lasting security.

I was very confused by this. What was preventing

women from being as powerful with money as they were in other areas of their life?

I have long said that self-worth determines one's net worth. When you are silent, or silenced, it's very hard to get in touch with your self-worth. *It is only when you speak your truth that you can be truly powerful.* Starting in the fall of 2017, women began to speak their truth, and it suddenly started to make sense to me.

When women in the entertainment industry bravely came forward and shared their experiences of sexual harassment, it was a harrowing, galvanizing moment. That was soon followed by widespread reports of women in media being mistreated. In early 2018 came the female athletes who were able to speak truth to the doctor who had abused them years earlier, when they were vulnerable children. A movement began—#metoo—and then another—#timesup.

Women who for years silently carried the ache of shame and fear were now courageously standing in their truth and speaking out. Other women were speaking out on behalf of wage equality and fairness in the workplace.

I am in awe of the women who have found their voices and are creating a safe space for others to speak up. They have ignited a national reckoning in which women are determined to demand more for themselves and from themselves. This movement will empower women for generations to come. There is no turning back.

It was against this backdrop of women engaging from a place of power and action that I decided now was the time to restart the conversation about women and money.

I truly believe that the promise of strength and security

that is at the heart of *Women & Money* is more timely now than ever before. I offer this book to all of you who are ready to step up, own your power, and take control of your financial life.

Let's get to work on building a life where you truly become the strong, smart, and secure women you were all born to be. That is my wish for each and every one of you.

Suze Orman
September 2018

WOMEN & MONEY

1

IMAGINE WHAT'S POSSIBLE

When *Women & Money* was first published it was my eighth book. All my previous books were written with the belief that gender is not a factor on any level in mastering the nuts and bolts of smart financial management. Women can invest, save, and handle debt just as well and skillfully as any man. I still believe that—why would anyone think differently?

So imagine my surprise when I learned that some of the people closest to me in my life were in the dark about their own finances. Clueless. Or, in some cases, willfully resisting doing what they knew needed to be done. I'm talking about smart, competent, accomplished women who present a face to the world that is pure confidence and capability. Do you mean to tell me that I, Suze Orman, who make my living solving the financial problems of total strangers, couldn't spot the trouble brewing so close to home? I don't think I'm blind; I just think that these women became very, very good at hiding their troubles from me. Why not? They had years of practice hiding them from themselves.

It began with a friend, a very high-powered business-woman who handles millions and millions of dollars a year, who refused to sign will and trust documents I'd helped her prepare. I can't tell you why, but those papers sat on her desk for *three years*—she clearly had some kind of block that prevented her from simply signing her name and having the documents notarized. Then another friend, a woman with some amazing professional credentials, broke down and confessed that she had rung up such staggering bills over the years that she was too terrified to tell anyone and had no idea how to pay them off. Not long after, I heard from yet another friend, who had finally woken up to the fact that her employer was paying her significantly less than every other executive of comparable rank in her company. Her division was one of the most profitable and consistent earners for the company, but still she just accepted the minimal increases her boss would hand her every year at review time.

Upon further investigation, I learned that so many women in my life—friends, acquaintances, readers, people who'd been fans of my TV show and appearances—all had this stumbling block in common: an "unknown factor" that prevented them from doing the right thing with their money.

Do you find yourself identifying with some of these emotions and actions? My experience is that if you are honest you will answer yes, and there are many reasons why you are choosing to hold yourself back.

Maybe it is your fear of the unknown; maybe precisely because you hold it together in every other part of your life you have a little streak of rebellion when it comes to money; or maybe you just feel that things have gotten so far out of hand you are embarrassed to ask for help and reveal just how much you don't know.

What is important to understand is that this stumbling block is exhibited not only by women in their 40s, 50s, and 60s but by women of all ages. Can I just act my age for a moment? I am 67 years old. I have lived through the transformation of women's roles at home, in society, and in the workplace. When I am with women in their 20s and 30s, what I love the most is that you aren't asking for equality; you expect it. You aren't doubting your talents relative to men; you know you've got what it takes. You seek relationships for their emotional possibilities, not their economic practicality. You don't need to be convinced of your worth; you own it. Loud and proud. Amazing.

Now, here's what I don't love: Like your mothers, aunts, and grandmothers, you share with me how confused and powerless you are with your money. You refuse to get involved with your money until some crisis occurs, and then you act out of fear.

Women of all ages have the horrible habit of thinking money is just too complicated to master. You give up without even trying. You could not be more wrong. It is not a question of intelligence. You absolutely have what it takes to understand what you should be doing.

A book with the title *Women & Money* must begin with

the story of how far women have come financially. It's not only a remarkable tale of social progress, it's a reminder for us that changes that take place on a personal level, every day in small doses, add up to dramatic societal and cultural shifts over time.

Women today make up nearly half of the total workforce in this country. Over the past 40 years, women's earnings have more than quadrupled. Women in the U.S. are the decision makers for about 40 percent of invested money; that works out to more than $11 trillion. Yes, trillion. Fifty-one percent of all professional and managerial-level workers are women. Women bring in half or more of the income in the majority of U.S. households. Women-owned businesses make up nearly 40 percent of all companies in the United States. There are more women than ever before who can count themselves among the country's millionaires, more women in upper management.

We have a right to be proud of our progress. I am so honored to witness this revolution in my lifetime. I only wish it told the whole truth.

Now, would you like to hear the other side of the story? Sixty percent of women worry about not having enough money to last through retirement. Five years ago nearly half of women surveyed were still expressing concern that they might run out of money and become homeless in retirement. Another survey reports that just one in five women say they are confident they can make smart financial choices. Nearly one-third of women expect Social Security to be their primary source of income in retirement, yet the typical monthly payout is less than $1,400. Did you know the poverty rate for women at least 65 years old is 40 percent higher than the rate for males?

For years now, I have been in the privileged position of talking to thousands of women a year. I hear, see, and feel your fears, insecurities, and troubles, very often firsthand, and I have come face-to-face with this painful truth: For all the advancements that women have made in the past 40 years—and without a doubt they are remarkable accomplishments—I am stunned by how little has really changed in the way so many women deal with money. There are huge disconnects at play here—between what we know and how we act; between what we think and what we say; between our ability as achievers and our financial underachieving; between how we present ourselves to the world and how we really feel about ourselves inside; between what we deserve in our lives and what we resign ourselves to; between the power we have within reach and the powerlessness that rules our actions.

In 1980, when I was hired as a financial advisor for Merrill Lynch, I was one of the few women in the Oakland, California, office. In the eyes of my (male) boss, that made me the perfect candidate to work with all the women who walked through the door. Back then, women who came to a brokerage firm looking for financial advice had, for the most part, inherited money, received it in a divorce, been widowed, or suddenly been thrust into a position of helping their parents handle their money. In only a few instances had women come in with money they'd made on their own. No matter the circumstances that brought them to the brokerage firm, they all had the same reason for being there: They did not want the responsibility of managing their money. I always felt they hired me simply to babysit their money for them.

Nearly 40 years later, the story is often much the same. Regardless of the gains in our financial status, I know and you know that many women still don't want to take responsibility when it comes to their money. Yes, women are making more money than ever before, but they are not making more of what they make. What do I mean by that? Your retirement money sits in cash because you haven't figured out how to invest it properly, so you do nothing. You've convinced yourself that you'll be working forever, so the value of each paycheck becomes meaningless—after all, there will always be another one. Your closet houses the wardrobe of a powerful and stylish woman, but the dirty secret is that your credit cards are maxed out and you don't know how you're going to pay them off. But it's not just about saving and investing. It's about not asking for a raise at work when you know you are being undervalued. It's about the fear and loathing you feel when it's time to pay the bills every month because you don't know exactly what you have, where it's going, and why there isn't more left when it's all said and done. It's about how you berate yourself all the time for not knowing more and doing more . . . yet you stay resigned to this feeling of helplessness and despair as time ticks away.

This problem, in my opinion, is enormous and pervasive and universal. It crosses all ages, all races, all tax brackets. Who can deny the fact that there is a fundamental block at work here that is preventing women from becoming as powerful as they are meant to be? Not me. I would be the first one to tell you that everything you need to know to secure your financial future, to educate yourself, to make your life easy—it's all out there. Yours for the asking. But you don't ask; you don't want to know.

I see this fundamental denial, this resistance, in so many women, no matter what they do, how they live, or where they are in their lives. I see you literally giving your money away rather than dealing with it. I see stay-at-home moms who work 24 hours a day and yet hand over all power and control to their husbands because they don't earn the money. I see successful single women who refuse to focus on what they need to do today to ensure their financial security years from now. I see women in second marriages who fail to protect the assets they accumulated before they remarried and who feel uncomfortable bringing up money issues with their new husbands. I see divorced women of all ages who go into full-blown panic mode when faced with the reality that they have no clue what money exists, what to do when they get their share of the settlement, and whether they will be able to maintain their lifestyle post-divorce. And the most heartbreaking of them all? I hear older women use words like *powerless* and *worthless* to describe themselves. These women are filled with regret when it comes to the way they've lived their financial lives.

So why do you all do this to yourselves? Why are you voluntarily committing financial suicide, and doing it with a smile on your face?

Let me put it another way: **Why is it that women who are so competent in all other areas of their lives cannot find the same competence when it comes to matters of money?**

I have asked this question—of myself and others—over and over. Of course, there is no one answer. After much contemplation, here is what I have come up with: The matter of women and money is clearly a complicated issue that has much to do with our history and traditions, both societal and familial. These deep-seated issues are major hurdles to overcome, major tides to turn—and that doesn't happen overnight. It can take generations to effect change of this magnitude in our daily behavior. We'll explore these issues in greater depth in the chapters ahead, because they are absolutely a root cause of this problem. But we'll have to look at this on a behavioral level, too, since traits that are fundamental to our nature clearly affect how we approach money as well.

Consider this: It's a generally accepted belief that nurturing comes as a basic instinct to women. We give of ourselves; we take care of our family, our friends, our colleagues. It's in our nature to nurture. Our inner nurturer reigns supreme.

But we don't take care of our money as well as we take care of spouses, partners, children, pets, plants, and whatever else is in our lives that we love and cherish. Why?

I want you to think about that question. The answer is critical to uncovering what is at work here and what is holding you back. So I'll ask it again: **Why don't we show our money the same care and attention that we shower on every other important relationship in our lives?**

Because we don't have a relationship with our money.

Correction: We do have a relationship with our money. It's just a totally dysfunctional one.

What holds you back is that you simply won't bring yourself to take care of yourself financially, especially if those actions compete with taking care of those you love. You do for everyone before you do for yourself.

Your nature is to nurture. You take care of everyone before you take care of yourself. Your kids, your parents, your spouse, your siblings, your colleagues, your pets. Everyone gets your full attention.

No matter how good your intentions may be, they are nonetheless draining you.

The challenge is to finally learn—and accept—that to be truly powerful in your life requires making money moves that work for you. You are never powerful in life until you are powerful with money. Now, I am not suggesting you replace nurturer with narcissist. I do not want you to discard your generosity or shed your supportive and kind nature. This book is not about becoming more by becoming more selfish. Far from it. I simply want you to give *to* yourself as much as you give *of* yourself. I want you to think about financial self-care.

So, then, let's turn this relationship theory around and ask ourselves the following question: In order to become competent and successful in handling our money, in order to become the fully responsible women we know we should be, what is required of us?

We have to develop a healthy, honest relationship with our money. And we have to see this relationship as a reflection of our relationship with ourselves.

I can't put it any more simply or emphatically: How we behave toward our money, how we treat our money, speaks volumes about how we perceive and value ourselves. If we aren't powerful with money, we aren't powerful period. What is at stake here is not just money—it's far bigger. This is about your sense of who you are and what you deserve. Lasting net worth comes only when you have a healthy and strong sense of self-worth. And, right now, the money disconnect—this dysfunctional relationship—is a barrier to both.

Once you fully appreciate this and hold it as an absolute truth, you will also understand that your destiny depends on the health of this relationship. Are you honestly prepared to roll the dice on this one? Or would you rather feel that you have the ability, the determination, the power, to make this relationship work—as surely as you know how to nurture and give care to all the people you love in your life?

How do you repair this relationship?

The same way you would repair any relationship that is damaged: by acknowledging your mistakes, taking responsibility, and resolving to act in a way that will bring about change for the better. In the case of you and your money, that means making smart and strong money moves, moves with the goal of making you feel more powerful and secure. If you show money the respect it deserves today and carry that through in all your actions, then one day, when you can no longer take care of it, your money will take care of you. Respecting your relationship with money, you see, is the key not only to your security and independence, but to your happiness as well.

———

Now let's talk about happiness for a moment.

The simple fact is that **nothing more directly affects your happiness than money**.

Oh, I know, some of you are just horrified by this notion, maybe even offended. *Suze, how could you?* Happiness is about all the things money can't buy—health, love, respect—right? Absolutely true—all of these are essential to a happy life. All are determined by who you are and not what you have. But the kind of happiness I am talking about is your quality of life—the ability to enjoy life, to live life to its fullest potential. And I challenge anyone to tell me that such things aren't factors in your overall happiness.

Let's just walk through this together. Yes, I know that your health and the health of your loved ones is paramount, but explain to me what would happen if, God forbid, any one of you fell ill. Wouldn't you want the best care that money can buy? Wouldn't you be grateful that you were in a good health plan? And isn't it money that puts the roof over your head, and money that allows you to move to a neighborhood with a great public school system? And money that allows you to retire early, or quit your job when you go back to school to pursue a new career?

In a survey I saw called "Authentic Happiness" there was not a single question or answer that contained the word *money*. Why is it that we are so reluctant to embrace the notion that money is a factor in determining our happiness? What bothers me about this is that I think it's a lie not to acknowledge the power that money has to make our lives better and happier. It's not a subject for polite company? Is that what you've been raised to believe? Well, I'm here to tell you that this isn't just a problem of semantics. I believe that this "conspiracy of silence" is another reason why so many women are in the dark about financial matters. I have often said that we must be careful of our words, for words become actions. Well, the opposite of that is true, too: Silence leads to inaction. We don't talk about money with our friends, our parents, our children. In a 2015 survey, four out of five women said they have a hard time talking about money with someone they are close to. Many of those women said it was just too personal. Seriously? You can dish and confide in your besties, you can overshare on social media, but talking about money is taboo—it's too personal? That's where we get in trouble. How are we supposed to teach our children, how are we supposed to educate ourselves, if there isn't a free and frank flow of information about money? Why do we behave so carelessly with our money? Would we do that if we believed our very happiness depended on it? Let me put it this way: If we persist in denying money its place in our lives, if we don't give it the respect it most certainly deserves, then it will surely lead to unhappiness.

I am asking you now to harness the incredible intelligence and competence that serve you so well in all the other aspects of your life and apply it to your money. Anyone who has it in them to run a household, run a company, run a department of a company, run a carpool, or run a marathon is fully equipped to take control here. Anyone who is a supportive and caring wife, partner, mother, sister, daughter, best friend, caretaker, aunt, grandmother, or colleague has all the skills necessary to forge a solid relationship with money and make the kind of smart money choices that will support rather than sabotage you. **That's what it means to be smart, strong, and secure: knowing what to do and what not to do—and having the conviction and confidence to go out and do it. Not just think about it. Or intend to do it next week or next month. To actually do it. Right now.**

Make that commitment to yourself first, and I will help you. And together, let's imagine what's possible when you do:

Imagine: What it feels like to be freed from the self-doubt that holds you down.

Imagine: Knowing that when you are more powerful with your money, you will have even more energy to flood your communities with your intelligence and generosity.

Imagine: Opening the credit card bill each month and knowing you will be able to pay it off.

Imagine: Knowing you have done everything to take care of your family if something happens to you.

Imagine: Staying in a relationship purely for love, not because you have no idea how you would make it financially on your own.

Imagine: Loving yourself enough to choose a partner you don't have to rescue.

Imagine: Owning your home outright—no more mortgage payments.

Imagine: Knowing you will be able to retire comfortably one day.

Imagine: Raising children who've learned from you the wisdom of living within your means, rather than living out of control.

Imagine: Knowing you have helped your parents live full lives, without fear or uncertainty, right to the end.

The thought of more powerful and confident women on the loose in our country makes me so hopeful. The payoff for your commitment will extend beyond your finances. Having a healthy relationship with money puts you in a position to have better relationships with everyone in your life. It all flows together. A woman who is more financially confident and secure is a happier woman. And a happier woman is going to be better able to nurture, share, and give support to all those in her life.

All of it is possible.

2

NO SHAME, NO BLAME

In order to build a healthy relationship with money, there are some attitudes I am going to ask you to cast off—forever. First among them are two of the heaviest weights women carry, invisible twin obstacles of our past: the burden of shame and the tendency to blame.

You don't feel confident in your knowledge of how money works, so you hide behind the shame of it, deferring decisions to others or staying stuck in a pattern of inaction. This is just as true for my 20-something friends as it is for their 50-, 60-, and 70-something mothers and grandmothers. You wrap yourself in the cloak of shame rather than reveal your shortcomings—you, after all, are a doer! You have to be all things to all people—mother, wife, dutiful daughter, supportive friend, amazing colleague (or entrepreneur), school volunteer, cheerleader at home and at work. No room to betray uncertainty in that picture! No time to learn, anyway—*who has the time?!* You're so busy. And besides, you tell yourself, *I probably should have learned that ages ago. When did everybody else learn this and not me?* Hmm, maybe you were absent that day. . . . At this point, it's simply too embarrassing to reveal the depths of what you do not know.

And where the mantle of shame stops, the tendency to blame kicks in. *It's not my fault!* you tell me. (a) Society (b) My parents (c) My husband/ex-husband (d) All of the above . . . held me back! Where were the role models? No one taught me, no one showed me how, money decisions were always made for me. Now, I'm not belittling these factors or making fun of you. There's a lot of legitimacy in these complaints. Long-standing traditions in society and in the home have not made it easy for women to get the financial education they need to become competent, in-formed participants in their own affairs. Even today, no one is going to hand it to you—you have to go get it for yourself. It amazes me that a person can go through twelve years of school, four years of college, and then on to graduate study, and nowhere along the way was she required to take a single class on personal finance.

But let me ask you this: Where does blame get you? The answer is *nowhere*. **Blame renders you powerless.** You must get past blame to become who you are meant to be. And what does shame do to you? **Shame only serves to hold you back.** This book is about facing forward, not staying stuck in the past. It is fine to understand how we got here, but the next breath must contain a resolve to move ahead into a future that looks entirely different, into a destiny that is all yours. I want you to use your past to propel you into your future, rather than keep you in the dark of what no longer exists.

Easy for you to say, Suze. Is that what you're thinking? Are you wondering how I could possibly know about your situation? After all, I'm rich! I have everything I need, everything I want. You're right—I'm rich. But that was not always the case. Do you think I was raised in a family that had money and paid for a fabulous education? Do you think I had an MBA from some fancy business school? Nothing could be further from the truth. Maybe you think I married money. Not true—in fact, I never got married until I was 59 (which is probably why I have money today!). Let me tell you where I came from and how I got here—so you will understand that there is no excuse, no amount of shame or blame, that can hold you back and keep you from becoming all you are meant to be and having all that you deserve.

SUZE'S STORY

When I was a little girl, I had a speech impediment. I couldn't pronounce my *r*'s, *s*'s, or *t*'s properly, so words such as *beautiful,* for example, came out as "boobital." To this day, if you listen closely when I speak, you can still hear it. Words like *fear* and *fair* and *bear* and *beer* sound the same, and a word like *shouldn't* comes out sounding like "shunt." Back then, because I couldn't speak well, I also couldn't read very well. In grammar school on the South Side of Chicago, I had to take reading exams, and would always score among the lowest in the class. One year a teacher decided that he would seat us according to our reading scores. There were my three best friends in the first three seats of the first row, while I was banished to the last seat in the sixth row. If I always secretly felt dumb, it was now officially confirmed for everyone to see. Talk about feeling ashamed.

This feeling that I couldn't make it scholastically continued to haunt me throughout high school and on into college. I knew I would never amount to anything, so why even bother to try? Nevertheless, in my family and in the families of my friends, it was a given that we'd all go to college. In my case, I knew that I would have to pay for college myself, because my parents were having a hard time with money. The only options for me were community college or a state school. I applied to the University of Illinois at Urbana-Champaign and to my amazement, even though I did not score well on my SATs, I was accepted. When I arrived, I met with a guidance counselor who asked me what I wanted to study. I told him that I wanted to become a brain surgeon. He looked at my grades and said, "I don't think so. You don't have what it takes. Why not try something easier?" I did a little investigation and found out that the easiest major was social work, so I signed up for that. Why not take the easy way out? Why try harder?

During my first year at the University of Illinois, I lived in the Florida Avenue Residences in room 222 and worked as a dishwasher in the dormitory's cafeteria seven days a week to pay the bills. In my second year, I shared a one-bedroom apartment off campus with two friends I had met in the dorm, Carole Morgan and Judy Jacklin. Judy had a hilarious boyfriend named John Belushi, and the four of us had quite the adventure for the next three years. (Yes, this is the very same John Belushi who went on to superstardom on *Saturday Night Live*. Judy and John got married and the rest is history, but that's a story for another book.)

I was supposed to graduate in 1973, but my degree was withheld because I hadn't fulfilled the language requirement. Once again, it was the shame of my grade-school years holding me back. If I had trouble with English, what made me think I could learn a foreign language? I decided to leave school without my degree. I wanted to see America. I wanted to see what a hill looked like . . . a mountain . . . the Grand Canyon!

I borrowed $1,500 from my brother to buy a Ford Econoline van and, with the help of my friend Mary Corlin (a great friend to this day), converted the van into a place I could sleep during the drive across country. I convinced three friends—Laurie, Sherry, and Vicky—to come with me; I was way too scared to try this on my own. With $300 and a converted van to my name, we set out to see America. Sherry and Vicky jumped out in Los Angeles, but Laurie and I continued on to Berkeley, California. As we drove through the hills on the day of our arrival, we were stopped by a man with a red flag who held up traffic so trees that had been cut down could be cleared. That year a frost in the Berkeley Hills killed many of the eucalyptus trees. I got out of the van to watch and walked up to the man with the red flag and asked him if they needed any help. He pointed me to the boss, and before we knew it, Laurie and I had landed our first jobs—working for Coley Tree Service for

$3.50 an hour. We worked as tree clearers for two months, living out of the van and using a friend's home nearby to shower.

When it was time to move on, I applied for a job as a waitress at the Buttercup Bakery, a great little place where we used to get our coffee. To my delight, I got the job. While I worked at the Buttercup, I faced up to my shame of not having finished college and took Spanish classes at Hayward State University. Finally, in 1976, I got my degree from the University of Illinois. I was an official college graduate, working as a waitress. I stayed at the Buttercup Bakery, where I made about $400 a month, until 1980, when I was 29 years old.

After six years of waitressing, I had this thought that I could be more than just a waitress. I wanted to own my own restaurant. I called up my parents and asked to borrow $20,000. My mom said, "Honey, where do you expect us to come up with this? We don't have that kind of money to give you." I should have known better than to ask for something I knew my parents didn't have to give away. There's nothing a parent wants more than to help a child realize a dream; I knew my mother would have done anything to help me, but she was powerless. I felt awful.

The next day at work, a man I had been waiting on for six years, Fred Hasbrook, noticed that I wasn't my usual cheerful self. "What's wrong, sunshine? You don't look happy," he said. I told Fred about having asked my parents for a $20,000 loan. Fred ate his breakfast and then talked to some of the other customers I'd been waiting on all those years. Before he left the restaurant, he came up to the counter and handed me a personal check for $2,000, a bunch of other checks and commitments from the other customers that totaled $50,000, and a note that read: THIS IS FOR PEOPLE LIKE YOU, SO THAT YOUR DREAMS CAN COME TRUE. TO BE PAID BACK IN TEN YEARS, IF YOU CAN, WITH NO INTEREST. I couldn't believe my eyes.

"I have to ask you a question," I said to Fred. "Are these checks going to bounce like all of mine do?"

"No, Suze," he said. "What I want you to do is to put this in a money market account at Merrill Lynch until you've raised enough money to open your restaurant."

"Fred," I said, "what is Merrill Lynch and what is a money market account?"

After a brief tutorial from Fred, I went to the Oakland office of Merrill Lynch to deposit the money. I was assigned to the broker of the day—the one who handled all the walk-in clients that day. My broker was named Randy. I told Randy the story of how I had come by this money and that it needed to stay safe and sound. I told Randy that I made only $400 a month as a waitress and that I needed to raise more money in order to open up my own business. He looked at me and said, "Suze, how would you like to make a quick hundred dollars a week?"

"You bet," I said. "That's about what I make as a waitress."

"Just sign here on the dotted line, and we'll see what we can do," he said. I did exactly what he asked, never thinking that it was stupid or dangerous for me to sign blank papers. Randy worked for Merrill Lynch, after all, and Fred said it was a great place to do business.

(Now, before I go any further, I just want to say that this is not a commentary on Merrill Lynch. Merrill Lynch is a fine, upstanding, and honest brokerage firm, but the bosses in the Oakland office had hired someone who didn't uphold their standards. If you have an account with Merrill or want to open up an account with Merrill, go right ahead; this particular bad seed is long gone. But more on that later. . . .)

It turned out that after I left that day, Randy had filled out the papers I had signed to make it look as if I could afford to risk the money I had deposited into the Merrill Lynch account. He got me into one of the more speculative investing strategies—buying options. At first, I was making great money. I was amazed. I found the perfect location for my restaurant and was having plans drawn up by an architect. My dream was within reach. Other people believed in me and lent me more money. We were off and running— that is, until the markets turned. Within three months, I'd lost all the money in the account. All of it. I didn't know what to do. I knew I owed a lot of money, and I knew I had no way to pay it back. I was still making only $400 a month!

During this time, I had been following what Randy was doing and was trying to learn as much as possible. I watched *Wall Street Week* on PBS every Friday night; I read *Barron's* and *The Wall Street Journal*. I taped the pages with the stock and option prices to my bedroom walls. After all the money was lost, I said to myself, *Hey, if Randy can be a broker, I can be a broker, too—after all, it seems like they just make people broker!* I got dressed in my best red-and-white-striped Sassoon pants, tucked them into my white cowboy boots, and put on a blue silk top. I thought I looked great! So did my friends at the Buttercup, who wished me luck as I set off for my job interview to become a stockbroker at the very office that had lost me all my money.

Five men interviewed me that day, and all of them asked why I had dressed that way. I told them I didn't know I wasn't supposed to dress this way. It wasn't as if there were lots of female role models I could learn from. Before I knew it, I was sitting before the branch manager, who looked as shocked as all the other brokers who'd just interviewed me. During the interview, he actually shared his belief that women belonged barefoot and pregnant. Seeing that I had nothing to lose, I asked him how much he'd pay me to get pregnant. He said, "Fifteen hundred dollars a month," and to my astonishment he hired me, though he also said that he figured I'd be out of there in six months. To this day, I am convinced I got the job only because he had a women's quota to fill. Before I left the office, I was handed a book on dressing for success. I took the book and went straight to Macy's, opened an account, and charged $3,000 worth of clothes.

I was never so scared in my life as that first day on the job. I knew I didn't belong there. All the stockbrokers drove Mercedeses, BMWs, and Jaguars. I drove a 1967 Volvo station wagon that I bought when I sold the van. They parked their cars in the parking lot; for the first six months, I parked my car on the street because I couldn't afford the lot. I would get tickets knowing that I'd go to court and ask to work the tickets off with community service. The other brokers would eat out at fancy restaurants after the market closed; I got in my car and went to Taco Bell every single day and ate by myself. Still, I felt so lucky and blessed, for even though I was terrified, I was also excited. Every day I was learning new words and concepts—a whole world was opening up to me. It was while studying to take my Series 7 exam, a test all brokers have to pass in order to sell stocks, that I read a rule stating that a broker needed to know his or her customer—meaning, a broker could not invest a person's money speculatively or risk their money if the customer could not afford to lose it. I had told Randy that I couldn't afford to lose my money, that I was saving up to open a business, that all the money was loaned to me. I realized that Randy had broken this "know your customer" rule.

I marched into the manager's office and told him that he had a crook working for him. He told me that I was a college graduate, and I had to know what I was doing when I signed those papers. Besides, he said, that crook made him a lot of money. He told me to sit down, shut my mouth, and keep studying. I went back to my desk. I remembered that when I was hired, the manager had told me I wouldn't last six months. That was just three months away. What did I have to lose? What had happened to me was not right. I had time to make that money back—I was still young—but what if Randy had done this to my mother or my grandmother or any older person? My conscience wouldn't let me keep quiet; I had to do something, for I knew it was better to do what was right than what was easy.

I ended up suing Merrill Lynch—while I worked for them. Now, what I hadn't realized at the time was that because I had sued them, they couldn't fire me. Who knew? Months and months passed as the case proceeded, and during that time I became one of the more successful brokers in the office. Before the lawsuit made it to court, Merrill ended up settling with me. They paid me back all the money plus interest, which allowed me to pay back all the people who had loaned me money.

Whenever I tell this story, people want to know what happened to Fred. When I repaid the money, it surprised me that I didn't hear from him. From time to time I would write or call and leave a message, but I never heard back. Then, in May of 1984, I got the following letter from Fred, who, it turned out, had suffered a stroke—the reason I hadn't heard from him all that time.

Dear Suze,

I had not intended to be this long in writing you a note of appreciation for your check repaying our loan from the Buttercup era.

However it seems that words don't come as easily to me as they once did. The check arrived at a critical time in my affairs and for that I am grateful.

That loan may have been one of the best investments that I will ever make. Who else could have invested in a counter girl with porcelain blue eyes and a million-dollar personality and watch that investment mature into a successful career woman who still has porcelain blue eyes and a million-dollar personality? How few investors have that opportunity?

I am working hard to get my affairs in order so that you and I can both make each other some money. Until then I would like to remain on your list of friends who wish you the very best of everything no matter what paths you may travel in the future.

Fondly,

Fred Hasbrook

Fred has passed away, but he will remain a part of my life forever. I'll never forget the man who believed in me, who helped me put aside my shame and rewrite the story history had handed me.

REWRITE THE STORY HISTORY HAS HANDED YOU

I tell you my story not to impress you but to inspire you. I want you to understand that it is not just our education or what society has handed us that determines what we can create for ourselves. It is how you decide to write your own story, how you decide to live your life.

There are countless examples throughout history and from various cultures of how women have been disinherited and disenfranchised, so it's no wonder that women today struggle with their money. It's a foreign experience. Throughout the ages, it was the man's job to bring money into the family. If you were to lay out a historical graph that charted women's evolution from non-earners to earners, our new roles as income producers would barely rate as a blip. These changes are that new.

And yet women have come so far so fast in the workplace since the beginning of the women's movement. Remember the statistics I cited in the last chapter? Who could have predicted such rapid, dramatic change in such a short time? At work, we have overthrown traditions that were centuries—millennia—old. So why is it that we haven't made the same evolutionary leap when it comes to our personal finances? When *Women & Money* was published in 2007, my explanation for how this could be leaned on traditions. Despite what was going on outside in the world, inside the home, traditional roles held tight. Those roles dictated that men handle the finances. Many successful career women at that time most likely had mothers who abdicated their role in major financial decisions to their husbands, as their grandmothers did and their great-grandmothers before them, the beat of history marching on. Today we have more women who grew up with mothers who were working outside of the home, many of them the sole or primary breadwinner. Yet women are still not finding it easy or natural to be powerful with their money. As I explained in the introduction, I believe this is because women—despite great progress—have been struggling in many other facets of their life to speak their truth and embrace their power. How we relate to money is a reflection of what we feel about ourselves. As far as women have come during my lifetime, there are still traditions, stigmas, and cultural biases to overcome.

The recent wave of women finding their voice—and being heard—makes me hopeful that women are entering a new stage of awareness and intent.

In keeping with my challenge that we use the past to propel us into a new future—that we rewrite the story that history has handed us—I am asking you now to see yourself as an agent of change in your own life and on a global scale. This change is necessary and urgent, given the world we live in today. Consider these realities of our twenty-first-century life:

- Retirement security is now your responsibility. Pensions have become rare, on their way to extinct, in the corporate world. The retirement plans now offered through work require you to step up and save some of your current salary, and to figure out exactly how to invest that money so it can support you decades from now. Neither task is easy. And please don't talk yourself into thinking you will be able to get by on Social Security. Social Security was never meant to be the primary source of retirement income. The average monthly benefit is around $1,400. How secure would your retirement be if that's all you had to pay your bills? What that means is that you are going to have to rely on yourself in retirement much, much more than your parents and grandparents did.
- With the divorce rate hovering around 40 percent, many women at some point in their lives will be solely responsible for managing their money. That also holds true for the increasingly larger segment of the female population who delay marriage or choose not to marry at all. Nearly one in five women over the age of 25 has never married, more than double the percentage in 1960. And, of course, this also includes the growing number of single-parent households.
- Even in the marriages that work, money is more of an issue than ever before, especially in homes where there is a stay-at-home mother—making ends meet on one income is a huge challenge these days. I can tell you that the only way to make it work—and I mean the marriage, not the finances—is for both partners to share responsibility

for the money decisions. Otherwise, you will be undone by money arguments.

- Women live longer than men. A 65-year-old woman today has an expected average life span that is nearly three years longer than a 65-year-old man. About one in three women age 65 and older lives on her own. The point is that the family finances will be your concern—and yours alone—at some juncture. The time to prepare for that is now. I have seen too much heartache, frustration, and costly financial mistakes made by women who are thrust into the job of financial manager later in life and have no interest or clue about what to do. I never want any of you to find yourself dealing with that fear and anxiety.

- We are also expected to live a lot longer than our parents or grandparents. At the same time, our mothers and fathers are also living longer. That's the good news, but it comes with additional responsibility. Your parents may well need your financial help to maintain their lifestyle as they age or to pay for care they could eventually need.

You get the idea. This isn't your grandmother's world anymore. We are trailblazers.

For the sake of all the mothers who came before you and for the sake of the daughters who will come after you, I'm calling on you to move out of the past and into the future, armed with knowledge and confidence. That means leaving behind old attitudes, old excuses, and tired alibis for not becoming as fully competent and able in the area of personal finance as you are in every other role you inhabit in your life. If you are asked to describe yourself without using the words *mother, grandmother,* or *daughter,* or your job title,

I want to hear you say, "I am powerful, I am secure, I am in control of my financial destiny."

No more hiding behind excuses. It's too easy to hide. No shame, no blame. Allowing shame to hold you back—too easy. Blaming others rather than taking responsibility for yourself—too easy. Today I am asking you to do what's right, not what's easy.

Building a New Relationship with Money

To build your new relationship with money, I am first going to ask you to do an exercise with me in which you will voyage back to your childhood. It is there that you will discover the foundation for your current relationship with money. We are all quick to acknowledge that experiences on the playground, in the classroom, and within the privacy of our childhood homes shaped who we are now. But we don't extend that to an appreciation of how our money memories continue to play a role in how we navigate the world today.

Your Money Memories

I am going to guide you to reconnecting with your earliest money experience. Those of you who have read my book *The 9 Steps to Financial Freedom* will recognize this exercise. It never fails to reveal profound truths about how we relate to money.

I want you to think back to your very first memory of money; when money represented something real to you. Don't think too hard about this. What is the very first thing that pops into your head?

A favorite present you received at 5? A present you didn't

receive at 12? A valuable lesson on the value of money from a grandparent or parent? The ache of hearing or sensing money arguments between your parents? Watching the financial fallout from your parents divorcing?

Once you identify your most powerful money memory, start writing. The more specific and honest you are, the stronger you will emerge. Do you remember what you were wearing that day, or what time of year it was? What was said, by whom? And what was not said that you so wish had been? What happened right before the memory? And after?

Facing Your Fears

It is my experience that when people embrace this exercise, they come to identify a money memory that is fraught with sadness, or anger, or shame. Those emotions keep you from being strong. They have festered for years, taking hold of your head and your heart as a fear.

When we live with fear, we are powerless. A money memory that continues to express itself as a fear you're carrying around today is what is between you and a secure future. And the fears we have from our childhood bleed into our adult life.

The next part of the exercise is to think about your greatest money fear in your life today. What are you afraid of? Do any of these fears resonate with you?

> I am afraid I won't be able to support myself in retirement and will become a burden to my children.
> I am afraid I may be laid off, and I don't know if I can get another job at this level.

I am afraid my kids don't understand that we can't afford to send them to their college of choice.

I am afraid that I won't be able to take care of my parents and my children and still be able to work.

I am afraid of all the things I need to do with my money, but I have no idea how to handle.

I am afraid I am staying in this relationship for financial reasons.

I am asking you to face your fear in order to move past it. This is the beginning of the path to becoming a strong, smart, and secure woman. When we live with fear, we are powerless. A money memory that continues to express itself as a fear today is what is between you and a secure future. The fears we have from our childhood bleed into our adult life. It is not until you break the chains that link you to your past that you can begin to create the future you deserve.

To move forward requires that you connect the dots between your earliest money memory and your greatest money fear. I will tell my story first, and I will show you how those two elements shaped my life.

My earliest money memory occurred on a hot Chicago summer day when I was 12. My friends invited me to go swimming at the Thunderbird Motel. I knew I needed money to be allowed into the motel pool, so I asked my mom for some money. She told me there was no money for that.

That my family didn't have the money for the pool immediately made me feel different from my friends. And not in a good way. In my young mind I decided my family was a failure so I must be a failure as well.

I was so upset. I was convinced that I was destined to

struggle my entire life just as my parents did. And my lack of money would forever be a divide between my friends and me. I was afraid that I would never fit in—because my family was poor. And that became my biggest fear.

So what did I do? I snuck around the house late at night, while my family slept, and stole money out of my dad's pants pockets. Then I would spend the stolen money on my friends. I was "dealing" with my fear of not fitting in by trying to buy my way into friendships.

Once I started working in high school, I continued to spend the money I earned on other people. And this behavior continued throughout college and my years of waitressing. The fear of not fitting in remained constant.

When I started working as a stockbroker at age 30, my money memory/fear was once again front and center: Fear of not belonging. Fear that everyone had money and I didn't. Fear that I would not succeed.

My earliest money memory, from age 12, was running my life at age 30.

Do you see how my money memory was related to my greatest fear?

Now see if you can find the connection between your earliest money memory and your most present money fear today.

Creating a New Truth

Once you have unearthed your money memory and connected it to your fear, you are ready to create a new money truth.

Let me tell you how I moved past my money fear.

As I mentioned, when I left my waitressing job to become a trainee at a stock brokerage, I was the proverbial fish out of water. It was the first time in my life I was not working a blue-collar job, and on top of that I was the only female trainee in the program. Fear was my sidekick: fear of being in a new and entirely foreign workplace, fear of sticking out, fear of not knowing if I could cut it. Absolute, total fear of failure.

Enough was enough. I knew I had to stop this debilitating fear from making me feel so vulnerable. That's when I created a new truth to silence my fear.

I decided I would talk myself out of my fear by envisioning the future self I was working so hard to create. My new truth was: *I am young, powerful, and successful, and I make at least $10,000 a month.* Notice I said "at least" $10,000.

Mind you, at the time I was 30 years old and I'd been earning $400 a month and living off of Taco Bell. But my new truth became my rallying cry. I repeated it multiple times each morning and before I nodded off at night. I forced myself to write it over and over and over. Whenever fear started to roil in my head, I drowned it out with my new truth. Fear was no longer my sidekick, success was! I know you can create the same powerful truth for yourself.

Your Turn

I want you to stare down your fear and write the new truth that will push your fear aside. A truth that is bursting with strength and confidence.

For example, if your fear is that you will never have enough money, your new truth can be *I have more money than I will ever need.*

I want you to create a short declarative statement that

you can memorize, so that repeating it at least 25 times a day is easy. I have two rules: Your truth must be in the present tense. "I have more money than I will ever need" is a declaration of power. Saying "I will have" or "I hope to be" or "I want to be" is not allowed. If you say "one day" I will have more money than I will ever need—who knows when that one day will be? Remember, too, that your statement of intent must not be self-limiting. In my truth I said "at least" $10,000. That's what I mean by not putting limits on yourself.

For the next six months you will:

• Write your truth 25 times a day.
• Say your truth out loud 25 times a day.
• Before you go to bed, look yourself in the mirror and silently speak your truth 25 times before you go to bed.

Our words have incredible power. What you say will eventually become what you believe. And your words become your actions. Those actions then become your habits, and that shapes your destiny. That is why I am asking you to write, think, and say your new truth repeatedly. Embracing your new truth throughout each day will lead you to the destiny you deserve, a future where you are the smart, strong, and secure woman you deserve to be.

3

YOU ARE NOT ON SALE

Change, I realize, doesn't happen overnight, especially when we are talking about traits and habits that have become embedded in our character, thanks to years and years of practice. It is the work of this chapter, then, to call out some particularly damaging forms of self-sabotage, not for the purpose of making you feel bad—remember, there is no shame or blame happening in these pages—but to convince you of the importance of making this attitude adjustment.

The attitude I am referring to is the tendency women have to undervalue themselves. Do you think I'm generalizing? I don't think so. I've got to tell you, I see this trait and its horrible side effects in action so often, it feels like an epidemic to me. So many women—from professionals to stay-at-home moms—treat themselves, their services, and their abilities as if they were always on sale.

I have always said that if you undervalue what you do, the world undervalues who you are. And when you undervalue who you are, the world undervalues what you do. My experience is that women are, unfortunately, masters at both.

All the women who are now passionately making their voices heard, standing up to harassment, marching for the world they want for themselves and their communities, running for office in record numbers, are women who are declaring their days of putting themselves on sale are over.

As that becomes our amazing new normal, women will also find themselves energized to bring that resolve to their relationship with money.

NO MORE DISCOUNTING YOURSELF

The big problem as I see it is that women treat themselves as a commodity whose price is set by others. That means women get to stand by and watch as their value is marked down, or not fully valued. Tell me if any of the following scenarios sound uncomfortably familiar to you:

- Your boss tells you that your raise will be 3 percent this year, and yet you know that business is going great, your division is a leader, and you deserve a raise that is at least double what you are getting. You, however, say nothing. You cannot bring yourself to ask for a raise that respects your accomplishments and your worth to the company.
- You have a successful business of your own. Your clients

love your work, so you get lots of referrals. But even though your operating costs have risen 10 percent in the past three years, you have yet to raise your prices. You are worried you will lose clients if you do. So instead of charging more, you take on a heavier workload to generate more revenue. You work yourself to the bone because you can't seem to value what you do, even though everyone tells you that you do it incredibly well.

• You are a stay-at-home mom. Your spouse works hard and brings home a decent paycheck. You're in charge of keeping the kitchen stocked and the house running, but when those expenses exceed what your spouse makes, it somehow becomes your fault. The problem is that as a family, you have expenses that exceed your income, but you allow yourself to become the sole party responsible for the problem. Even worse is the common division of labor I see in far too many marriages. The wife handles the day-to-day bill paying and the husband makes all the long-term planning decisions. It is scary how many smart, capable women take no role in understanding and driving their long-term financial security. They have no clue how much is being saved for retirement, how it is being invested, whether there is ample life insurance, and if they possess the key estate-planning documents to protect themselves and their children.

• You are a massage therapist, a manicurist, a haircutter. You are doing well and making good money. Yet every time a friend or business associate suggests a barter deal in which you swap services "for free," you agree to it. You don't really want to barter—in fact, you don't particularly want the services you will receive in the "trade"—but still you say yes because you are afraid of offending the other person. Bartering doesn't pay the rent or pay down your credit card bill, but for some reason you just can't say no.

• You have a full-time job and a full-time family that needs your attention, but when the PTA asks you to help organize the school auction, you sign on. They know they can count on you; every time you are asked to volunteer, you oblige. Volunteering is just what women do, right? It comes with the territory. . . .

Did you find yourself in there somewhere? Do you get it? You treat yourself like you're on sale. You're so reluctant to put a real value on what you do that it diminishes who you are. And as I said, that creates a vicious cycle: When you devalue what you do, it becomes inevitable that you—and those around you—devalue who you are.

When I ask women who run their own businesses why they refuse to raise their prices, they tell me they are afraid to make their needs a priority. When I wonder why a woman who's been a loyal, productive employee doesn't push her boss for a meaningful raise, it becomes clear to me that she's intent on being the good soldier at work. One difference between when this book was first published in 2007 and today is that we are beginning to see women increasingly holding their bosses accountable for gender pay inequities. The conversation is occurring more and more; true change for all women will come only if we individually and collectively make it clear we will not let our employers put us, and keep us, on sale.

When I see a stay-at-home mom acting as if her husband's paycheck is his and not theirs, I see a woman who does not appreciate the very valuable job of running a household and raising a family.

You need to take yourself off the sale rack. Once you learn to respect your right to be fully valued, you will find it easy and natural to ask the world around you to respect that value. You set your price, and the world will meet it. When you walk through the world feeling you are "more than" rather than "less than," more will come to you. No one ever achieved financial security by being weak and scared. Confidence is contagious; it will bring more into your life.

It's also important to recognize that your time has value. What I see far too often is that women say yes to giving without calculating the cost of that decision. If you had to put a price on your time, you'd have to take into account the emotional toll and the financial toll of what you are giving away. The financial price is obvious: Are you being compensated fairly for your time? The emotional price is what it takes out of you when you say yes. Too often, both of these measures are overlooked when you are called upon to volunteer, which leads us to . . .

THE VOLUNTEER SYNDROME

It never fails that when I participate in a women's conference or meeting, there is one speaker who makes the point that volunteering is terrifically important for women. It is always the same message: We owe it to society to give back, and we owe it to our children to set a good example of giving back. The audience always nods eagerly in agreement. Now, here is what I find fascinating. I have never once—and I mean not once—heard a male speaker make that point. Men talk about power and success and how money can create more power. Men are comfortable with that. Women are so uncomfortable with the topic of becoming powerful and successful that they have to wrap any discussion of it in the comforting blanket of volunteerism. What is that about? This is not a comment on men; it is simply an observation of what men are told versus what women are told. Again, this is why we have to blast open our past and let it go.

Do men volunteer? Of course. But not in the same way. Men sit on boards, men coach Little League. Women, on the other hand, bake pies, organize the school auction, chaperone field trips. Generally speaking, women tend to take on the more labor- and time-intensive behind-the-scenes tasks. Also, the fact is that more women volunteer than men. According to a government survey, 28 percent of women volunteer compared to 22 percent of men.

If it's not encoded in our DNA, then it is certainly the result of the traditional roles of days gone by. Men went off to work; women tended to the home front and created community. Men donated money; women didn't have money of their own to give away, so they gave time. Look at your own life and tell me if this still holds true. My guess is it probably does not, which means that an adjustment of expectations—collectively—is in order.

Now, I want to be very clear here. I am not suggesting that every minute of every day you must be "on the clock" or that you should never volunteer your time. That is *so* not my message, I cannot even tell you. Being powerful is not about being selfish, but it does require that you examine your behavior and see where you may be out of balance. And when you do make the decision to donate your time and your effort, know the true worth of what you are giving.

THE BARTERING TRAP

Can you tell me why it is that so many self-employed women find it hard to charge for their services? The minute a friend, business associate, or even a total stranger suggests they "swap" services, the woman agrees. Again, this is not in itself a bad thing to do, but only if you can afford to barter. If you need cash to pay the rent or fund your Roth IRA, then why are you agreeing to swap two hours of your consulting services for one hour of someone else's public relations expertise?

Money is not dirty. Wanting and needing money is not wrong. When you have a healthy relationship with money, you understand its value and importance in building the secure life you seek for yourself and your family. Do not put your time and services on sale—or up for barter—until you are sure you have the money you need to take care of yourself. Money first, barter second. That's the Right Action/ Right Relationship.

Now, if you do barter, I want you to make sure that it is a fair swap. If your time is worth $100 an hour—since that is what you charge your paying clients—but your friend who wants to barter does work that is valued at $50 an hour, you are not to do an even-up one-hour swap. You have just devalued yourself again: You are bartering at a rate that is 50 percent below what your time is worth. If you are consciously cutting a deal with your friend because you want to help her out, then that is okay—but again, only if you can really afford to bestow that gift. If you give someone a $50-per-hour break on your work and you give them one hour of your time a week, that is $200 a month you are not making for yourself. If you have high-rate credit card debt, that's $200 you are giving away to someone else rather than getting out of debt. So don't then tell me you can't find the money to invest in a Roth IRA; you just gave away $200. And by the way, if you invested that $200 a month in your Roth IRA every year for the next twenty years, it would grow to more than $80,000, assuming an average 5 percent annual return.

Eye-opening, isn't it? So please be mindful of the cost of bartering. If you can truly afford to barter, great. But don't make it a default position that you always say yes. Or that you always agree to whatever terms the other party has suggested. When you undervalue what you do, the world undervalues who you are. That's the antithesis of owning the power to control your destiny.

RAISE YOUR EXPECTATIONS

Given what I do for a living, women are quick to bare their financial lives to me. I love listening, I always try to offer advice when advice is asked for, and in return I am constantly learning how women think and feel about money. Want to know what I see all the time? Women too scared to demand to be paid what they are worth. From stay-at-home moms to executives overseeing multimillion-dollar budgets who get measly raises, to the massage therapist or manicurist afraid to increase her rates, this condition is rampant, and it is a shameful secret women keep, too embarrassed even to tell their closest friends. Luckily, they tend to confess such things to me.

Here's one story: I know a massage therapist who is so fabulous, she is very much in demand. Recently, she told me, she was called by a woman who had injured her back. She told the woman that her rate was $80 an hour. The woman thought that was too pricey. "I'll pay you $60 an hour," she told my friend. Do you know what my friend the massage therapist did? She lowered her price to $70 an hour. The woman objected that the price was still too high but agreed, reluctantly, and made an appointment. On the day of the appointment, as my friend was on her way to the woman's house, her cellphone rang. It was the woman— canceling the appointment.

Now, let's look at this. One would tend to blame the woman—how rude that she broke the appointment, how cheap, and so on. But no—the massage therapist brought this on herself. I told her just that. She put herself on sale; when she marked herself down, she invited the woman to bargain with her. What if my friend had the power to say, "Listen, actually I'm worth even more than $80, so that's my price, take it or leave it," and the woman had left it? What would have happened? She could have filled that slot with someone willing to pay her full price. She could have saved herself the useless trip out to the woman's house. Or better yet—the woman would have respected her conviction, said fine, and kept the appointment. She'd have loved how she felt afterward and not only made more appointments, but she'd tell everyone she knew how great this massage therapist was.

Listen, I get that people want a bargain. There's nothing wrong with that. But putting yourself on sale is another story. You do that to yourself—no one is doing it to you. You are not a victim of circumstance; in a case like this, you create the circumstance. You can choose to be powerful or powerless. Remember, that choice is always yours.

Here's another story: A friend who works for a major corporation called to tell me she had been approached by a competitor and offered essentially the same job she was doing for her longtime employer, but at nearly double the salary. She was shocked and furious. In that instant, she realized how out of whack her salary was with industry standards and that her employer had been taking advantage of her for years. "This is how you get rewarded for your loyalty," she complained.

My advice to her: Go to the boss and let her know it was time to renegotiate their deal. But first, I told my friend, she had to let go of her anger and realize that she was complicit in this. She had permitted her employer to take advantage of her all this time. I asked her, "Did you really have no idea that you were making so much less than you should have been making?"

She thought for a moment, then said, "I guess a part of me knew, but I figured we were all in this together. I couldn't imagine that this woman I respected and did good work for would not reward me to the extent she was able. I believed her when she talked about belt-tightening."

"And yet you knew your division was making huge profits, right?" I asked.

She realized how naïve she sounded. Still, she needed to take responsibility for her role in this. I said, "You go in there and say, 'I realize that I have allowed myself to be unfairly compensated in the past, but now I'd like to correct that and be paid in a way that matches both industry standards and my division's profitability.' "

The lesson here is that you cannot assume that if you simply do good work you will be correctly compensated for your effort. Maybe some of you have truly enlightened bosses who are always quick to give you raises that reflect your effort and your value to the company, but that's not typical. In fact, it's downright rare. This is one area where women can learn from men. Men like to negotiate; men want to negotiate. Rustle some corporate feathers? Hey, a man's gotta do what a man's gotta do.

So many women are made intensely uncomfortable by the thought of having to negotiate their salary. Research shows that women are 2.5 times more likely than men to say they feel "a great deal of apprehension" about negotiating. In one study, men used the metaphor of "winning a ballgame" to describe negotiating, while women picked the metaphor of "going to the dentist." Hmm, a game to be won versus a painful experience . . . The difference in that perspective can cost women a lot. In the book *Women Don't Ask: Negotiation and the Gender Divide,* authors Linda Babcock and Sara Laschever estimate that an unwillingness to negotiate the salary at your first job can end up costing you an estimated $500,000 in lifetime earnings. And it turns out that men are four times as likely to negotiate. In another book, *Get Paid What You're Worth,* two business academics, Robin Pinkley and Gregory Northcraft, estimate that a woman who actively negotiated her salary over the course of her career could potentially earn $1 million more than if she just settled for what her boss offered. It's pretty clear: If you don't ask—and make a compelling case for a raise—you have little chance of getting what you deserve.

Here is how to make sure you aren't putting yourself on sale when it comes to your salary:

- **Be proactive.** The most important step is to recognize that you need to make this happen. Getting more requires asking for more. If you are not getting what you deserve, you are not to blame your situation on someone else or some external situation. You are responsible for valuing yourself and stating that value to the world. This holds equally true for employees of companies large and small as well as artists and stay-at-home moms.
- **Be impatient.** I do not want you sitting around waiting for your boss to magically appear and tell you the company is promoting you and giving you a raise. Take that approach and you could well be waiting a long time. I am not recommending you ask for a raise six months into a job. Be realistic. But if you have gone a long time—say, two years or more—and haven't received a raise, it's time to take action.
- **Be prepared.** Tell your boss you want to set up a meeting to discuss your compensation. Prior to that meeting, you are to give your boss a one-page outline of your achievements. Not ten pages, one page. The idea is that you are stating in clear terms what value you have brought to the company and why now is the time for the company to show that it values your effort. The words that should never come out of your mouth are: *I deserve a raise because I haven't had one in two years.* If I were your boss, that wouldn't do much for me. But if you state all the ways you

have met and exceeded expectations, then you have my attention. The fact that you value what you do causes a nice chain reaction. It gives you the confidence to state your case, and it then makes it difficult for your boss to undervalue your work.

- **Those of you who are self-employed, of course, have a different dynamic to deal with.** You aren't asking a boss for a raise; you are asking your clients for a raise. That seems to send women off the deep end; you would rather sit in an ice bath than discuss new rates with your clients. Do not apologize for raising your rates. Do not sheepishly ask for the increase. You are to tell your clients what your new rate is. You are a businesswoman—emphasis on the business. This is a business decision you are communicating to your clients. They don't have to pay that rate; they can indeed look for other options. But if you are good at what you do and you value your talent, they will not leave. If they do, know that you will be able to find new clients who will pay you what you know you are worth.

Okay, so what if you ask for the raise and your boss looks at you with doleful eyes and says, "I wish I could do more for you, but really, my hands are tied. All I can give you is a standard three percent increase this year, because that's the company's policy." Your boss is appealing to your kindness, hoping you will understand that money is tight, that maybe "next year" will be better. Do you just walk away without gaining anything? Usually you do, right? The female need to be liked, to be seen as a "team player," and your reluctance to speak up for what you deserve cause you to just take whatever your boss says as gospel.

Generosity is a two-way street. If being generous (in spirit, in patience) with your boss isn't being kind to yourself, then you are not acting powerfully. So, no matter how uncomfortable your boss tries to make you feel, I want you to stay right in your seat and keep the conversation going. If you know the company is on shaky financial ground, then of course you have to take that into consideration. But if the company is profitable, and you are in fact a contributor to that profit, then you are not to walk out empty-handed. Ask for a review and salary discussion in six months—not a year, but six months. In the meantime, if you can't get more salary, negotiate more vacation time. You must get something of value, for you are not on sale. I have to tell you that if your boss keeps coming back to you with measly raises and new excuses, you need to move on. I know switching jobs is not necessarily easy, nor is it a quick process. But if you work for an employer who does not value what you do, you need to go work for someone who does. When you value yourself enough to reject a bad situation, you are being powerful, and that power will motivate you to find a better job.

THE PURSUIT OF HAPPINESS:
AN EMAIL FROM MY FRIEND DEBRA

Dear Suze,

Remember when you and I first met a few years ago? You came to address a conference being sponsored by the big Silicon Valley company where I worked. On a break you and I got to talking. I told you that I was considering buying the condo I was renting, and the first question you asked me was whether I was happy in my job. I was so shocked at the question. What did that have to do with me buying a condo? You told me that until I found a job that made me happy, I shouldn't buy anything, because it was the down payment money I had in my savings account that would give me the freedom to make the move in pursuit of a job that I loved. The answer was so simple, yet it took you asking me about my state of happiness for me to see the light.

You also inspired me to ask for more money the next time I was offered a menial raise from my boss. I had been in my job for nine months when the performance reviews were due just before Christmas. When he called me into his office that week, we spoke for a good twenty minutes (that's a long time for him!) and he expressed how as each day passed, things got better and better and that he was very pleased to have me working for him. Then he presented me with a raise that was the equivalent of mice nuts. I had taken a $3,000 cut in my base pay to work for him, thinking once he saw my work ethic and level of dedication, he would reward it. Well, the joke was on me.

After the holidays, I approached my boss and made him aware that I was glad he was happy with my performance, but I was quite disappointed in the pay increase. I decided that I wasn't going to back down from asking for more—and didn't—and after three months of going back and forth, he finally gave me the increase I was asking for and made it retroactive! I was so proud of myself for finally standing up for me. It's taken me forever to get to a point where I would do such a thing—my god—I'm going to be 47 in February! But I did it—and it felt really good. So thank you for being such an inspiration to me, in my life, in ways that you are completely unaware of.

Yours,

Debra

Your goal is that from this day forward, you will consciously pay attention to what you need to be paid to feel powerful in your life and secure about your finances. You are to set your value, communicate that value to the outside world, and then not settle for less. Sound daunting? That's just because it takes you out of your comfort zone. You have got to stop being an obstacle on your own path to wealth and security and happiness. You must understand that valuing yourself is well within your control. Do not let others dictate your worth. You are never to put yourself on sale again.

4

THE EIGHT QUALITIES OF
A WEALTHY WOMAN

Now that we've gained some insight into the external forces that tend to make women feel powerless when it comes to matters of money, it is time to learn how to re-condition ourselves from the inside. What's required now is that we come from a different place within our beings so that we can realize the potential we all have to become powerful and wealthy.

A wealthy woman absolutely has money, but she also has harmony, balance, courage, generosity, happiness, wisdom, cleanliness, and beauty. A wealthy woman has it all, so to speak, and brings these qualities into every relationship, carries them with her in every waking moment of her life.

It's my wish that you will carry these essential qualities within you wherever you go and that they will serve as your guideposts to make sure you are always walking toward wealth rather than walking away from it. It is important you understand that all eight qualities must be present and work together at all times in order to attain and maintain the true state of a wealthy woman.

| Harmony | Balance | Courage | Generosity |
| Happiness | Wisdom | Cleanliness | Beauty |

QUALITIES 1 AND 2: HARMONY AND BALANCE

Harmony is an agreement in feeling, approach, and sympathy. It is the pleasing interaction between what you think, feel, say, and do.

Balance is a state of emotional and rational stability in which you are calm and able to make sound decisions and judgments.

Harmony and balance are perhaps the most important qualities of all, for they serve as the foundation for the remaining qualities. When you possess true inner harmony, what you think, say, feel, and do are one. We are so accustomed to this split-screen state of mind in which we think one thing, say another, feel something else, and act in a way that has nothing to do with what we just thought, said, or felt. When your thoughts, feelings, words, and actions are not in harmony, it shows up as an imbalance—you feel agitated, uncomfortable, you sense something is off, so you find it difficult to make rational, calm decisions. This is why these two qualities are a pair.

To make sure these two qualities are present in your life,

you need to pay attention to your feelings. Observe and listen to the words you use—the actions that you take should be perfect reflections of the thoughts you think. If you maintain this awareness, you will notice when you are out of harmony/balance. When you detect an imbalance, you are to stop whatever it is you are about to say or do and investigate the location of it. Take note when you feel agitated—it's a sign of impairment. If you read the definition of balance again—*a state of emotional and rational stability in which you are calm and able to make sound decisions and judgments*—you will understand that it is an essential cornerstone to a lifetime of correct and powerful behavior.

QUALITY 3: COURAGE

Courage is the ability to face danger, difficulty, uncertainty, or pain without being overcome by fear or being deflected from a chosen course of action.

Courage gives harmony expression. When your thoughts and feelings are one, courage helps you manifest them in the form of words and actions. When you are afraid to speak or act, courage helps you overcome your fear. Courage gives you the ability to speak your truth, even when it is not what others may want to hear. Courage is what helps you find your voice.

It can be difficult for women to connect to their courage. Women can be deflected from a course of action if they think that it might hurt someone else. We've seen how corrosive it can be to remain silent, to silence ourselves, even if we've been wronged, because we're afraid of upsetting others or upending the status quo. The #metoo and #timesup movements have shown us the toll that silence takes, and they have inspired women from all walks of life to come forward and speak their truth.

It's so much easier to hurt yourself than to hurt someone else, isn't it? Women also lose their courage when they subscribe to a belief that someone or something is the key to their happiness—rather than recognizing that power lies within.

If you are dependent on your husband or partner to support you, it is easy to lack the courage to speak up on behalf of yourself and your family. Think about it: Are you willing to risk the roof over your head for your needs and wishes?

Fear is usually what stands between us and our courage. We're afraid to rock the boat. We're afraid of confrontation. We're afraid to upset someone. We're afraid we'll lose our job. We're afraid he will divorce us. We're afraid our kids won't love us. We're afraid of what others may think of us. We're afraid we will be flat broke. As we explored in the Money Memory exercise, we carry fears borne from childhood experiences of loss or anxiety. Often those childhood memories have nothing to do with money per se, but when we become adults, the lingering emotional connection to that experience manifests itself as a money fear. The list goes on and on.

Living with fear is not just sad, it is exhausting. I have never met anyone living with fear who is able to keep it at arm's length. When we experience fear, it seems to invade us at a cellular level that we carry with us everywhere, all the time. We can't tune it out.

If we are to embrace this quality of courage to its fullest, we can no longer allow ourselves to live with fear. I hope you are already feeling emboldened by the money memory exercise that begins on page 32. I want you to know that courage is a muscle that needs to be flexed throughout your life. Long after I had achieved professional success, I was reminded of this powerful truth.

SUZE'S STORY

There was a time when it appeared that everything was right in my life. I had three *New York Times* bestsellers, I was on television, I had money, I had fame, and I was doing good, helping people connect to their money and improve their financial lives. I was surrounded by family and a circle of friends and colleagues I was close to . . . and yet something wasn't right. Though in *The Courage to Be Rich* I had written about the need for thoughts, feelings, words, and actions to be one, it took some time for me to locate the source of the imbalance in my own life. I came to see that I had a few friends and professional colleagues who truly did not have my best interests at heart. Though on the surface we appeared close, the truth was, we were not. I seemed always to be serving their needs, responding to their schedules, paying attention to what they were doing, while they showed little interest in where my life was taking me—unless it was useful to them in getting ahead in their own careers. If asked, at the time, I would have said I loved them, but in truth, I sure didn't like them, not on any level. And because I had been afraid to speak these thoughts— even to myself—and act upon them, I was robbing myself of my happiness, my power, and my self-respect.

One day, I decided that needed to change. I needed to muster up all of my courage to squelch my fear and to act on what I had been feeling, yet was too afraid to acknowledge, for years now. I took a seriously deep breath and proceeded to do some very dramatic housecleaning. Within a few hours—literally—I ended every one of those relationships once and for all. For the first time in years, I was truly in harmony and balance. I felt proud of myself; despite my fear, I had acted in a way that was true to myself, and the reward was the harmony and balance I was now feeling.

To this day, it remains one of the best things I have ever done. I did an internal housecleaning and made space for other people to come into my life. And when the right people entered my life, it started to soar. I had relationships that were based on truth. I felt the benefits of harmony and balance internally, and I also became more powerful. I had awakened courage that had been dormant, and it started to show up all over the place. The more I used it, the more readily it was there to help me, and my life grew bigger, better, happier, and richer.

QUALITY 4: GENEROSITY

Generosity is when you give the right thing to the right person at the right time—and it benefits both of you.

Generosity is a quality that most women can tap into very easily—maybe too easily, if you ask me. As women, we tend to be overly generous with our time, support, love, and money—but giving simply for the sake of giving does not match the definition of true generosity as stated above.

True generosity goes far beyond what you give to others. In giving there is a power, an understanding that you are just the vessel that wealth or energy flows through. You allow money to come in through your hands and out through your heart. To be empowered to give, to be moved to give straight from the heart, is a feeling that all the money in the world could never buy. That is how I want you to feel when you have been truly generous.

So let me ask you: Is that how you feel when you constantly give of yourself? Do you feel enhanced or do you feel diminished? Be honest here. You think of yourself as a giver, as generous with your time, your talent, your compassion, your patience, your money. Others probably describe you as a generous woman, but if I were to look at you, I might think you give for the wrong reasons. Do you give because you feel that you should? Do you give to feel included? Do you give out of guilt or embarrassment? Do you give because you're worried about what others will think if you don't?

It is very important that you understand that *true generosity is as much about the one who gives as it is about the one who receives.* If an act of generosity benefits the receiver but saps the giver, then it is not true generosity in my book.

To me, honest giving must always observe these six rules:

1. **You give to say thank-you and out of pure love. Not to get something back.** A true gift has no expectations on it or demands.

2. **Whether it is a gift of time, money, or love, you must feel strongly that your gift is an offering.** It should be given freely and out of pure love.

3. **An act of generosity must never adversely affect the giver.** When you give money that you honestly can't afford to give, that gift adversely affects you.

4. **An act of generosity must be made consciously.** You must be aware of how your gift will affect its recipient and make sure it will not be a burden.

5. **An act of generosity must happen at the right time.** You must be able to afford to give your gift, whether it is a material item or the gift of time.

6. **An act of generosity must come from an empathetic heart.** Your generosity should be directed to those who move your heart, those you feel need your help and will treasure the help you give. Giving should enhance you, not diminish you.

QUALITY 5: HAPPINESS

Happiness is a state of well-being and contentment.

When you find the courage to live your life in harmony and balance, when you understand and practice generosity in the truest sense, happiness spontaneously appears.

When you are happy, you are open and accessible. When you are happy, you tend to be more optimistic. You approach new challenges with a clear mind that seeks positive solutions. You see possibilities rather than problems.

If you are not happy, then I would ask you to try to find the place in your life where there is discord and not harmony. Have you wanted to do or say something but failed to find the courage to act? Have you been too giving or generous for the wrong reasons? When you are unhappy, you feel as if something is missing in your life—and that something becomes a hole to be filled. It is dangerous to be in a state of wanting, for it leads to decisions that are not always made with your long-term best interest in mind.

Happiness is not a luxury. It is a necessity for true wealth. When you are happy, you find pure joy in your life. You are not in a state of wanting but a state of contentment. You have the satisfaction of knowing that your actions come from a place of purity and balance, that they are correct and generous and kind. There are no regrets in this state of happiness—and that's a goal worth striving for in all areas of your life.

QUALITY 6: WISDOM

Wisdom is the knowledge and experience needed to make sensible decisions and judgments, or the good sense shown by the decisions and judgments made from an accumulated knowledge of life that has been gained through experience.

The quality of wisdom is more than intellectual, and it is in no way related to how much schooling you have. Exercising wisdom requires cutting through the noise of life and tapping into your core beliefs to make thoughtful decisions. Wisdom results from inhabiting all the qualities that came before it. A wise woman recognizes when her life is out of balance and summons the courage to act to correct it. A wise woman knows the meaning of true generosity. A wise woman knows happiness is the reward for a life lived in harmony, with courage and grace. A wise woman knows how to summon her courage and do what is right, rather than what is easy.

QUALITY 7: CLEANLINESS

Cleanliness is a state of purity, clarity, and precision.

Cleanliness is about respecting the importance of order and organization. When you don't know where your money is, when you have no filing system for your important documents, when you dive into your pocketbook to pull out crumpled bills, when your car looks like a garbage can, when your closets are filled with junk and clutter—I'm sorry, but you cannot possibly be a wealthy woman.

You need to clean up your act—quite literally—to bring true wealth into your life. In India, women sweep the front entrance to their home each morning as a way of welcoming Lakshmi, the goddess of material and spiritual abundance, into their home, for there is a belief that she resides at the threshold of every house. In order for her to enter, she must have a clear path.

Start with your pocketbook and wallet and make sure all bills face the same way and that every morning you put them in order. Next, donate clothing you have not used or worn in the past twelve months to a charity of your choice. Simply throw out all the beauty products that go unused. Remember, when you keep things around you that are worthless to you, they end up making you worthless.

Are your important documents organized? They should

be. When your accounts are clean and orderly, you can find the information you need to make good decisions.

You might be reading this and thinking that cleanliness is nice but not essential to your financial well-being. I am here to tell you that if this quality is not up front and center, and if you do not adhere to it, there is no way you will ever own the power to control your destiny. Wealth will elude you, and you will be left with the mess that you created. Respect the power of this quality of cleanliness. Make it your way of honoring the goddess Lakshmi, if only symbolically. Tell the universe that you have cleared the path for wealth and abundance to enter.

QUALITY 8: BEAUTY

Beauty is the quality or aggregate of qualities in a person that gives pleasure to the senses or pleasurably exalts the mind or spirit.

Beauty is what you create when you incorporate the other seven qualities into your life. When you take the steps to have harmony, balance, courage, generosity, happiness, wisdom, cleanliness, and beauty in your life, you will exude confidence in who you are. And there is nothing more beautiful than a confident woman. Remember, when you are confident you feel secure, and when you feel secure you have no fear. And when you have no fear, you have the courage to say what you think and feel in a calm and wise way. And when you are calm, you make wise decisions with your money, which then allows you to be truly generous to others as well as yourself, which, in turn, makes you a happy, powerful, and beautiful woman. Do you see how all of these qualities work together to help you arrive at the goal of being a woman in control of her destiny?

SUMMONING THE EIGHT ESSENTIAL QUALITIES

I've noticed, in my own life and in others', that the more you summon these qualities, the easier they are to access. Harmony yearns for more harmony, and balance abhors imbalance. Courage begets greater courage. Once you are generous in the right way, a lesser form of generosity will feel inferior to you. True happiness will never permit you to settle for a lesser form of happiness.

Carry these qualities with you throughout your life. Write them on a note card and keep them close at hand—in your wallet or in your pocket. Make it into a talisman to guide you every day as you make your way through life and all its impossible demands. These qualities will keep you focused and tranquil. Let them in and they will offer you constant reassurance that you are acting powerfully and correctly, with love in your heart and the purest intentions, to realize your goals of security and comfort for yourself and all you love.

Harmony	**Balance**	**Courage**	**Generosity**
Happiness	**Wisdom**	**Cleanliness**	**Beauty**

5

THE FINANCIAL EMPOWERMENT PLAN

When it comes to money, and why we have not done what we know we should, we can endlessly debate *why this* and *why that* until we are all blue in the face. We can make sure that you are thinking the right thoughts and saying the right words, but at the end of the day you have to stop talking and just start doing.

We are at that point. So far, all the learning in this book has awakened you to the opportunity for calm and strength that awaits those who can reengineer their relationship with money. Now you are ready to become that woman who is smart, strong, and secure.

Are you still afraid? If you are, that's okay, but there is only one way to conquer fear, and that is through action. That's why I devised The Financial Empowerment Plan.

In updating the plan for this edition, I have edited out a lot of the extensive explanations that were in the original version. I know you are time-crunched. I know you are smart and capable, but you don't necessarily have the time or motivation to take a deep dive into the *whys* and *how comes* behind every financial move I am asking you to make. You want to do the right thing but need someone to clearly spell out what that entails with step-by-step guidance.

I hear you. I have reworked the plan to be as streamlined as possible. What follows is not me explaining, or cajoling, or cheerleading. This is not Personal Finance 101.

This pared-down Financial Empowerment Plan is me telling you exactly what you need to do to be smart, strong, and secure. Period. The plan is all about simplicity. If you want to learn more about a particular topic, you can take my online Personal Finance course, for free. Go to SuzeU .com/activate and use the activation code MONEY.

We will focus on four central goals:

I. Protect yourself. We start with the steps to protect yourself, and your family. Building an emergency fund protects you from today's unknowns. Your tomorrows are protected with life insurance and making sure you have drawn up the essential documents, such as a revocable living trust.

II. Spend smart. The road to financial security is paved with decades of smart borrowing decisions. This is how to spend smart on big-ticket expenses.

III. Build your future. I know the subject of retirement planning is daunting; there are so many moving parts to juggle, it is easy to give up before you even start. That's not what you will encounter here. I have pared down the advice to the essential steps to take to achieve long-term security.

IV. Give to others. You will see how to build healthy money relationships with those you love. And the how-tos for financial planning with a spouse or partner, raising money-smart kids, helping adult children find their financial footing, and knowing when to say yes and when to say no.

My hope is that you will read through the plan from start to finish. I understand the temptation to fly past sections you think you don't need to read because you have already taken care of that topic in your own life. Or because you have let someone else—a husband, partner, brother, uncle, financial advisor—take care of it for you, and they assure you everything is "in order." I don't care if Warren Buffett is your financial advisor. Power doesn't come from relying on someone else to handle your money. It is created when you—and only you—take the initiative to learn about your money and to make sure that you have what you need. That's my definition of power. And it's as much about reviewing what you already have as it is about taking new steps to build security.

The Financial Empowerment Plan requires a total buy-in. There is no lasting security if you just cherry-pick the items that you think you want to tackle right now or that you feel are important. Every item I have called out in the plan is a necessary piece of the puzzle that, when finished, will reveal a new you: smart, strong, and secure.

YOU CAN'T BE SMART, STRONG, AND SECURE UNTIL YOU TACKLE CREDIT CARD DEBT

The Financial Empowerment Plan details every move you must take to stand tall, in your truth, and be a powerful woman in control of her money and her life. But I can't get you there if you are currently struggling in the financial quicksand of credit card bills that you can't pay off every month.

I hate to break it to you, but if you have credit card debt, you are not ready to begin this plan. You must first get yourself on solid financial ground by once and for all tackling your fraught relationship with credit cards.

That starts with an honest assessment of why you have unpaid credit card bills. It is understandable—and yes, acceptable—if your credit card debt is a result of a truly unforeseen emergency, such as medical expenses. But my experience is that many people with credit card debt simply spend too much.

Credit card debt is often a signal of irresponsibly living above your means. You say yes to yourself after a long day—or week—and indulge in some retail therapy. You say yes to the kids' latest request because you just can't find your way to being honest with them, or you're too tired to confront the consequences of saying no. You spend more than you can honestly afford to impress people, be it your work colleagues who have a habit of picking too-expensive lunch spots, or people you don't even know. What's up with the $400 monthly car payment?

I'd also ask you to take an honest look at what your

excess spending has truly bought you. Are you happy having spent the money the way you did? I bet there are plenty of regrets hanging in your closet, or in boxes tucked under your bed or in your garage. The cost of those purchases exceeds their price tag. That was money that didn't go into an emergency savings fund or a retirement savings account, or toward a down payment on a home.

I am not interested in assigning shame or blame. The past is past. That you are reading this book—and find yourself at this page—tells me you are ready to change, to embark on a new path.

I have two interactive tools on my website that can help you tackle your credit card debt and become more conscious of your spending, so you never run up new balances you can't pay off.

My Expense Tracker will help you take a clear-eyed view of your spending, making it easier to recognize what is a need versus what is a want. Trim spending from wants and you will have more money to put toward paying down credit card debt.

My Debt Eliminator tool will show how to tackle your credit card debt, what to pay off first, and how to see it through until your balance owed is zero.

You can access both the Expense Tracker and Debt Eliminator by going to suzeorman.com/women and using the activation code WOMEN.

I. PROTECT YOURSELF

Step 1: Build an Emergency Fund

Building a financially secure life starts with laying a foundation that will support you when the unexpected happens. You and I both know life frequently goes off script. One month it's a car repair, the next an unplanned medical test with a hefty copay, or the need to hop on a plane to visit an ailing relative.

An emergency savings fund is not just a foundation you need. It is the foundation you deserve. Do you understand that shift in approach? This is not a horrible, burdensome thing I'm asking you to do. I'm asking you to commit to creating a situation that gives you security and peace of mind—which in turn will empower you to make the right choices, knowing that you have a safety net. An emergency savings fund will transform your life. Imagine waking up each day knowing that no matter what comes at you, you've got it covered. You don't have to worry about overdrawing your checking account, or racking up expensive credit card debt. Being freed from that worry is liberating beyond anything you can imagine.

Ready to give yourself peace of mind? Let's get started.

A few years ago, my spouse, Kathy "KT" Travis, and I walked a long stretch of the Camino de Santiago in Spain. As we set out on our hundred-mile journey, I wasn't entirely sure we would reach our final destination. This was going to be a challenge! We not only made it, we had the experience of a lifetime. Reaching our final destination was exhilarating; a sense of accomplishment that has stayed with us. I went from doubting myself to wanting to do it again and again! Often KT and I find ourselves reminiscing about the journey. Each day, each step that moved us forward—it was an experience that we cherished. I want you to approach building an emergency savings fund as your own journey, propelled step-by-step by your deliberate decision to move forward and build the security you deserve.

Ideally, I want you to build an emergency fund that can cover eight months of living expenses. I am very much aware that this is a big ask. I know it will take time to save up so much money. Please try not to get frustrated or impatient. How long it takes you to reach your goal is not what's important. The triumph of smart decisions that you make every day is what should be celebrated. Every step moves you toward a strong and secure future. Every step is its own powerful declaration of intent.

I recommend an eight-month reserve so you will have maximum protection from whatever storms may form. If you are laid off or you have a serious illness, having just two or three months of savings is not enough—it will compound your stress. What if you need more time to get back on your feet? Eight months is a safety cushion that can truly protect you.

How Much Will You Need?

Write down how much money you need each month to pay all your essential bills (mortgage, utilities, food, insurance premiums, etc.):

> Monthly Cash Needed (MCN) $_____
> Multiply your MCN by 8 to set your Emergency Fund Goal:
> _____ x 8 = _____ = your Emergency Fund Goal

Set a Monthly Savings Goal to Build Your Emergency Fund

> Divide your Emergency Fund Goal by 12: $_____
> Divide your Goal by 24: $_____
> Divide your Goal by 36: $_____
> Divide your Goal by 48: $_____
> Divide your Goal by 60: $_____

It is up to you if you want to aim to build your fund in one year (divide by 12) or five years (divide by 60). Choose the amount that you can commit to saving each and every month. I encourage you to push yourself a little bit here. Start with a higher goal than what feels "easy." You can always adjust it lower if you need to.

YOUR SAVINGS PLEDGE

I'm asking you to commit to saving in a real, meaningful way, with these words:

"I am ready to stop worrying about how I will handle unexpected—but inevitable—expenses. I am going to save $_____ a month for _____ months."

A Narrow Definition of Emergency

Now that you are motivated to build an emergency fund, let's talk about how and when you should tap it. I want you to stop and have a heartfelt conversation with yourself before you ever withdraw money from your emergency savings fund. Will the money be used to provide an essential household need? To fix the car so you can get to work? The large out-of-pocket when someone becomes sick or injured? The rent or mortgage payment when you get laid off and need a few months to find your next job? Those are fantastic reasons to tap your emergency fund. Giving money to your child who wants to go away for spring break or doesn't have the down payment for a car is not essential. Nor is loaning them the money. Remember the quality of generosity. It needs to be generous for you. When you reduce your emergency savings fund below eight months to help out someone else, you are putting your future in jeopardy. That should always be done only as a last resort, and for a need that is essential to that person's well-being. Vacations, nice cars, business ventures do not qualify.

Don't Think About It. Do It.

I bet you have long wanted to build an emergency savings fund. You have always had the intention to do this for yourself. But as we often experience in our lives, intention does not always easily lead to action. Especially when you are asking yourself to forgo something today (spending) so you can have something for the future (more financial security). Who naturally gravitates toward delayed gratification?

I can help here. The trick is to automate your savings. The easiest way to get up and running is to open a new savings account at the bank or credit union where you already have a checking account and set up a recurring transfer from the checking account to your new, liberating emergency savings fund.

Log on to whatever bank or credit union you use. (Or call customer service.)

Open a new savings account. I insist that your emergency fund be a separate account. Your emergency money should never be kept in your regular checking account.

Set up a monthly automatic transfer from your checking account into this new savings account. (If you prefer bi-weekly or weekly, that's fine. Whatever feels right to you.) This service will be free.

Name your emergency savings account. Many online accounts allow you to rename them to whatever you'd like. Researchers have found that personalizing an account and calling out its purpose and your intent can help with motivation to keep saving and spending it wisely. I want you to choose a name that inspires you. Every time you log in to your account I want you to be reminded of the amazing step you are taking to protect yourself. ReadyforAnything. IAmAwesome. NoMoreWorries.

Step 2: Consider Life Insurance

I know . . . you just want to skip right past this step. Life insurance is a topic that triggers all sorts of flight responses. You're forced to acknowledge your own mortality and envision the well-being of your loved ones after you have died.

But I am also sure that if you open yourself to this challenge, you will be amazed at the positive energy and calm that will come from relieving such a huge psychic burden.

Just imagine the liberating feeling of knowing that your family will be financially okay if anything should happen to you. None of us can control our time here. Yet we all have the opportunity to plan for our loved ones' security. I can think of no smarter decision or stronger declaration of protection than to make sure the financial future of the people you love is secure, no matter what.

I will be the last person ever to suggest that money can heal a family after a loss. But leaving loved ones in a financial lurch compounds their grief and can have lifelong repercussions.

Life insurance is a final financial gift so that your loved ones can focus on being their best selves. Life insurance is what allows your family to carry on, with the least amount of logistical disruption. It can help them stay in the house or pay for the college you have all been dreaming of. Life insurance makes a good life for your loved ones more attainable. It is a thoughtful act of caregiving that extends your love and support beyond your lifetime.

I understand if part of your dread is the notion of having to deal with a pushy life insurance agent that you're not sure you can trust. Relax. Buying life insurance can now be a low-hassle endeavor.

I am going to walk you through exactly what you need—and don't need—and you will be able to shop for life insurance online without any sales pressure. I will recommend a few online companies you might want to consider working with. You can fill out an application online, and then sit back while the company "shops" your situation among a few insurers and comes back to you with a few solid leads to companies you might want to work with.

After you decide which insurer you want, you'll fill out a more detailed application with the insurer. Depending on the size of the policy you choose, you may need to schedule a time for a medical tech to stop by your home or office to draw some blood and take your vital signs. No doctor visit! They come to you—for free.

Quick Quiz: Do You Need Life Insurance?

Let's first determine if you need, or a spouse or partner needs, life insurance.

Is anyone dependent on you financially? **Yes   No**

If **No:** You may not need life insurance. I hope you will keep reading this section of The Financial Empowerment Plan to make sure.

If **Yes:** Answer this question:

If you died tomorrow, would your assets provide enough income to support your loved ones for as long as needed? **Yes   No**

If **Yes:** You may not need life insurance. I encourage you to review the rest of this part of The Financial Empowerment Plan to be certain that you understand all the variables in making sure your loved ones will be fully protected for a long time, not just one or two years.

If **No:** You need life insurance.

Are you dependent on anyone's income? **Yes   No**

If **Yes:** You better make sure that person has life insurance and you are a beneficiary. Continue to the next section.

If **No:** You may not need life insurance. But please be sure to review the advice in the rest of this section of The Financial Empowerment Plan to be absolutely sure.

ADVICE FOR STAY-AT-HOME PARENTS

One of the most dangerous mistakes families make is to insure only the breadwinner. As a matter of fact, it is just as important to have a life insurance policy that covers the stay-at-home parent, too. Think it through logically for a moment: If the stay-at-home spouse were to die, and there were young children, the surviving spouse would probably need to hire someone to care for the kids. Where is that money going to come from? Even if your children are in their teens, help from a homework tutor or a driver to transport them to and from sports practices, music lessons, and so on, may be necessary. Remember, your partner or spouse can't be expected to work a full-time job and help 100 percent of the time with the needs of the children. The proceeds from the life insurance policy will enable a surviving partner or spouse to hire caregivers without the worry of spending "extra" money. I recommend you work up an estimate of what the annual cost would be to hire a team to support your family. Multiply that sum by the number of years until your last kid is out the door. That's how much life insurance you need.

Decide Which Type of Life Insurance Is Best for You

Many life insurance agents will try to sell you on the idea that you need to buy a super-expensive policy that will cover you throughout your entire life. The reality is that very few of us ever need a "forever" life insurance policy—what the industry often refers to as a permanent policy.

Whole life is one example of permanent insurance. This type is unnecessary and way too expensive.

Life insurance is meant to provide financial protection for those who are dependent on you at a point in your life when you have yet to build up other assets. Once you have accumulated assets that your dependents can fall back on—say, a sizable retirement fund or other significant investments—you no longer need life insurance.

Besides, people dependent on you today may not be dependent on you in ten or twenty years. A 5-year-old child today is completely dependent on you. But twenty years from now, I expect—and so should you!—that your 25-year-old child will no longer rely on you for significant financial support. (Please note: If in fact you have dependents with special needs and you anticipate that they will require your support forever, you may indeed want to consider a "permanent" type of life insurance. You should also talk to a lawyer who specializes in estate planning about setting up a special-needs trust.)

Therefore, for most of you, if the primary purpose of your life insurance is to protect young children you anticipate will grow into independent adults, then you probably do not need a policy that is longer than twenty to twenty-five years, max. Same goes with life insurance for a spouse or partner; chances are you only need to provide protection until the assets you both have accumulated have grown large enough to support the surviving spouse if one of you should die prematurely.

Q: How long do you need life insurance to protect your loved ones?

☐ A. For 25 years or less

☐ B. Forever

If you checked A: You need a term life insurance policy. This is the type of life insurance the vast majority of you will need. The rest of this section of The Financial Empowerment Plan will walk you through everything you need to know to purchase the best term life insurance policy.

If you checked B: You may need a permanent life insurance policy. I recommend consulting with an attorney who specializes in special-needs trusts and estate planning. That's the first step before focusing on which type of permanent life insurance policy is best.

Term Insurance Key Words

Okay, so we've made a lot of progress. You are ready to add this important piece of the financial puzzle to protect your loved ones. And we are going to focus on term life insurance. I think you will be surprised how straightforward the process is. All you need to know are four key concepts:

Term: Refers to how long your policy will last. Term life insurance can be for one year, five years, 10 years, 20 years, even longer.

Beneficiaries: The people who will be paid by your life insurance policy if you die during the term.

Death benefit: The amount of money that will be paid to your beneficiary(ies.) For example, a $500,000 life insurance policy has a $500,000 death benefit. In the event the insured person dies while the policy is active (what's called "in force" by insurance types), the beneficiaries of the policy will receive a $500,000 payout from the policy. A death-benefit payout is typically tax-free.

Premium: The annual cost to pay for your coverage. Just like homeowner's insurance or renter's insurance. As long as you keep paying the premium, you are covered. I want you to ask for a "level term policy." This kind of policy has a premium that will never change; the premium you pay in the first year will be the same as the premium in the last year.

Calculate How Big a Death Benefit You Want

One way to calculate the size policy you want is to focus on the current income of the person you will be insuring. However, I am going to suggest you take a slightly different approach. I want you to consider a policy that would cover your family's total living expenses. It's an added layer of protection that will give the surviving family members more financial flexibility in case they don't want to—or can't—continue to work at their previous pace.

What are your family's monthly living costs?_____

You want to add in everything: Mortgage/rent. Property tax. Utilities. Insurance premiums. Food. Vacations. After-school classes and sports. Babysitters. Haircuts. Movies. Meals Out. Etc.

If you go to my website, you can use my Expense Tracker to help you figure out your monthly living costs. Go suzeorman.com/women and use the activation code OMEN.

> 1a: Multiply your monthly living costs by 12:_____ = annual living costs.
>
> 1b: Multiply 1a by 25:_____ = your preliminary death benefit target.
>
> (Example: If your annual living costs are $50,000, multiply that by 25: = $1.25 million.)

The Rule of 25: I want you to multiply your living costs by 25 because ideally your beneficiaries should be able to live off the interest of your life insurance policy without having to touch the principal. At some point, your beneficiaries may want to use the principal, maybe to help the next generation with their financial goals. But in the near-term, knowing they can live off the interest and not have to dip into the principal will provide tremendous peace of mind.

If you have young children and you want to help them attend college, let's add those future bills to your death benefit calculation. Here are some estimates on average costs based on a child's current age. Your costs may end up being less, once grants and financial aid are factored in, but let's play it safe and plan based on typical costs before financial aid.

Current Age of Child	Future Total Cost of 4-year In-state School	Future Total Cost of 4-year Private College
Under 10	$185,000	$420,000
10–15	$110,000	$245,000
16 and up:	$100,000	$225,000

Source: Vanguard College Cost Projector, vanguard.wealthmsi.com/collcost.php.
Estimates include tuition, fees, room and board.

College Bill for Child 1: $_____
College Bill for Child 2: $_____
College Bill for Child 3: $_____
College Bill for Child 4: $_____
Total Potential College Costs: $_____

Add your target death benefit from 1b and your total potential college costs:

_____ + _____ = _____
Base Death Benefit   College Costs   Your Death Benefit

Okay, I bet that looks like an incredibly daunting sum. Stick with me here. Term life insurance is affordable. Below are a few examples of annual premiums based on the current age of the insured. These examples are for a nonsmoker in good—though not triathlon-ready—physical shape. Your health will impact your premiums.

Annual Premium Costs for a 20-Year Term
Life Insurance Policy

	Death Benefit	
	$1.25 million	**$2 million**
Male 35 years old	$950	$1,500
Female 35 years old	$825	$1,300
Male 45 years old	$2,200	$3,600
Female 45 years old	$1,750	$2,800

Again, these are annual costs. The $3,600 for a $2 million policy for a 45-year-old male works out to $300 a month. I respect that the amount is not nothing, but it's also buying you $2 million of peace of mind! You can always scale back your death benefit to a sum that will give you an affordable premium. But in a world where the average car loan payment is more than $400 a month, I would ask you to consider trimming your savings elsewhere—stop buying such expensive cars!—so you can easily handle a term life insurance policy with a death benefit that will provide incredible protection for your family.

Create Your Shopping List

You're ready to pull it all together and start shopping for a term life insurance policy. Here's what you will want to ask for:

A level term policy for _____ years.
A death benefit of $_____.

You only want quotes from insurers with a financial strength rating of *A* or better. You can ask the company helping you shop for life insurance to provide each candidate's financial strength rating.

Start Shopping

You can always check with the insurer who handles your homeowner's or renter's insurance to get a quote. But realize that's just one company. If you want to shop among multiple insurers, these sites work with more than one insurer.

Accuquote.com
PolicyGenius.com
Quotacy.com
Selectquote.com

All of these sites will work with you closely from start to finish, serving as the liaison between you and the insurance company.

Sign Up for Auto-Payment

If the insurer offers a way for you to automate payment of your premium, that is the smart way to go. This is one bill you do not want to let slip. If possible, pay it annually to avoid a service fee of $5 or so per payment if you pay monthly or quarterly.

Step 3: Create Your Must-Have Documents

This next step is, in my opinion, the most liberating, empowering . . . and the most emotionally demanding. I am asking you to put in place the paperwork that will serve as the operating manual for your family to step in and take care of you if you become too ill to express your wishes. We are also going to make sure you have streamlined the process for how to pass on your assets when you die. How you help your family navigate these emotionally challenging events will be a part of your legacy.

Not the easiest of topics, I know. But if they go unaddressed, these deeply rooted fears will gnaw at you. What if you get sick? Who will take care of you? Who will take care of the kids? When you die, are there likely to be family eruptions over who gets what, when? You may love each member of your family with every cell of your being, but that does not mean they will not have disagreements. Especially if you die without spelling out your wishes.

While none of us can ultimately control fate, we can have a tremendous say in how we navigate illness, and how easy (or hard) we make it for our loved ones to follow our wishes. To summon the courage to create essential documents, such as a will and revocable living trust, is to give you and your family an amazing gift.

The Family Protection Plan

The term *estate planning* does little to encourage or motivate. So let's reframe this for what it really is: protecting yourself and protecting your family. Estate planning is simply taking care of stuff today so that when tomorrow comes, your family doesn't need to think, or decide, or argue. It just needs to follow what you've laid out.

Decide Which Documents You Want

Check any of these that are important to you:

☐ 1. I have a clear preference about wanting to be put on or taken off of life support.

☐ 2. I want to avoid family arguments and have one person convey my health care wishes if at any point I am unable to express them for myself.

☐ 3. I have children who are minors.

☐ 4. I want to make it as easy as possible for someone I appoint to step in and handle my bills and finances if I am no longer able to handle these tasks.

☐ 5. When I die, I want my investment accounts and other assets to transfer to my loved ones—exactly as I have spelled out—in a fast and inexpensive way.

☐ 6. I have some keepsakes that I want to make sure pass to specific people when I die.

IF YOU CHECKED #1:

YOU SHOULD CREATE AN ADVANCE DIRECTIVE

What it does: This document clearly spells out the level of medical intervention you want in the event you become too ill to speak for yourself. A range of situations is addressed, including consenting to or refusing any care or treatment, such as pain relief; selecting health care providers and institutions; approving procedures; and directing end-of-life decisions, such as organ donation and providing or withholding nutrition and resuscitation. In essence, you are giving directions in advance, while you are able to make sound decisions, to your doctors or medical team. An advance directive is also known as a living will.

IF YOU CHECKED #2: YOU SHOULD CREATE A

DURABLE POWER OF ATTORNEY FOR HEALTH CARE

What it does: Now, the hard truth is that an advance directive/living will does not guarantee that doctors will automatically follow your wishes. Surveys of doctors and medical students have shown that there is much confusion in the medical community about how to interpret an advance directive. This is an excruciatingly difficult area for everyone to navigate—you, your loved ones, your doctors. In such situations, your durable power of attorney for health care becomes your voice.

In a DPOA for health care, you appoint someone you trust to become your agent in the event your illness prevents you from communicating your wishes. This person will literally speak for you, representing the wishes detailed in your advance directive in any discussions and debates with your doctors or family. You can appoint anyone to be your agent—a spouse, a friend, an adult child. I only ask that you think this choice through carefully. You want your agent to be not only someone you trust, but also a person who will be able to represent your wishes faithfully, even in the face of objections from family or medical advisors. You also want this person to want to do this job. I have been asked to be an agent by many people I am close to, but I declined; I knew I couldn't make the tough decisions that might need to be made one day.

Once you settle on your agent and that person has agreed to do it, I strongly urge you to discuss this with your entire family. Let them know that you have an advance directive, and that you have appointed so-and-so as your agent. This will help reduce the hurt and anger that often crop up when families are brought together in a tragedy and first learn of the existence of an advance directive and an agent. Discussing it ahead of time will also help your friends and family present a united front to your doctors.

IF YOU CHECKED #3, #4, OR #5: YOU SHOULD CREATE A REVOCABLE LIVING TRUST WITH AN INCAPACITY CLAUSE

Of all the must-have documents, a revocable living trust is the most powerful, for, if set up correctly, it can take care of everything for you, both while you are alive and after your death. A will only kicks in after you die.

A trust is where you explain how you want a guardian to use your estate to care for a child who is a minor.

You can place certain assets inside your revocable living trust—called funding the trust. Your house can go in the trust; certain investment accounts can go in the trust. As long as you are alive and the trustee of your trust, you call

all the shots on managing those assets. And the revocable part means you have a ton of control and flexibility. You can move assets in and out of the trust, spend money in the trust, change your beneficiaries or the stipulations for when your beneficiaries are to receive an inheritance. You are always in control.

But let's say at some point you become unable to handle things. You succumb to a debilitating illness or dementia. This is where the trust becomes the savior for you and your loved ones. As long as your trust includes an incapacity clause, someone you have appointed will be able to quickly step in and handle your finances for you. I also recommend that you have a durable power of attorney for finances; many financial institutions require this document to be able to access retirement accounts.

That's why a will is not enough. A trust is how you en-sure your family can step in—if and when it is necessary—without having to hire a lawyer and go to court to get legal permission to handle your finances.

When you die, a trust delivers another important bene-fit. With a trust, your family does not have to deal with probate, a legal process in which an estate that is passing from a deceased person to her heirs must get a judge's ap-proval in a court proceeding. When you have only a will, your heirs may end up going to a probate court. That can cost plenty of time and money.

With a revocable living trust, your family will not be required to go through the probate process. When you cre-ate a revocable living trust, you will name someone as your successor trustee. That person will take over the trust when you die, and follow the instructions you have left as to when and to whom your assets should be dispersed. There is no need to get court approval.

IF YOU CHECKED #6: YOU SHOULD HAVE A WILL

While your trust takes care of your big-ticket assets as well as a potential incapacity, you no doubt have plenty of smaller assets that you want to pass along. Your grandparents' china, a treasured pen, a favorite set of earrings. A will is where you spell out who you wish to inherit these items. Your will also takes care of any assets that you didn't get around to transferring into the trust. Those assets will pour over to the will and be managed or disbursed exactly as you have laid out in the trust. That's why when you have a revocable living trust, your will becomes known as a pour-over will.

Drafting Your Must-Have Documents

If you are ready to put a few hours into protecting yourself and your family, I will help you create your must-have documents.

I am offering all readers of *Women & Money* my Must-Have Documents kit for $69. This program will help you create all the must-have documents you'll need, and it includes advice that is specific to each state. My own estate attorney, Janet Dobrovolny, worked with me to create this program. It includes audio and text coaching from me that explains everything in language a non-lawyer can understand.

Hiring an estate attorney to draw up these documents can cost thousands of dollars. I'd like to help you do this in an affordable way. Go to suzeorman.com/women.

II. SPEND SMART

In this section of The Financial Empowerment Plan, I will show you how to tackle big-ticket purchases: home, car, college.

Each has its own specific strategy, built around a shared reality. For most people, these purchases will require borrowing money.

I have no issue with borrowing money, if it is done carefully, responsibly, cautiously.

Yet what I see happening all too often is that you borrow based on the advice of someone who does not care one iota about your future. You turn to a mortgage lender to tell you how big a home loan you will be able to qualify for. You jump when the financing desk at the auto dealership shows you a loan or lease that makes the unaffordable suddenly seem affordable. You accept the financial aid plan from your child's chosen college as reasonable, without carefully assessing whether a lot of that "aid" is actually loans the school expects you and your child to take out.

The problem is that in each purchase, no one is looking at the big picture—your big picture.

The mortgage lender doesn't care if your monthly payment will be so big you won't be able to save as much as you would like for retirement.

The auto lender sure doesn't care that you will be overspending on a purchase that loses value from day one, when some of that money could be better spent on building financial security, such as adding to your emergency fund or paying down your other debts.

The job of colleges is to give your child the tools for creating a successful future, but the cost often undermines that very future for parents. Financial aid packages routinely assume parents will borrow to pay for school, yet the financial aid office has no obligation (or incentive) to point out whether parents can afford to borrow. We have a national epidemic of parents who have borrowed so much, they can't save enough for retirement. They can't pay off their mortgage before they retire. They are left exposed in their 60s, needing to keep working at a high-powered career in a world that is not exactly kind to older employees.

None of that is your fault. It is human nature to rely on others when we are unsure of ourselves. Or to defer to "experts." Nonetheless, your future, your family's ability to thrive decades from now, requires that you step up to the challenge of becoming your own best counsel on how to borrow for big-ticket purchases. Being smart and strong in how you spend your money is the foundation of the security you crave—right now, today, and in the future.

That's what we're going to tackle now: how to borrow smart.

For all the specific nitty-gritty advice that follows—specific to each loan type—there is one unifying principle to being a smart borrower:

Live below your means, but within your needs.

When you focus on borrowing the least amount possible that will provide for your needs, you are creating more financial breathing space. A smaller mortgage, car payment, or college loan balance gives you more freedom to build financial security.

That $100 or $200 a month less in a car payment becomes a way to turbocharge your emergency savings. The family decision for a child to attend a state school that does not require the family to take on a burdensome level of loans will enable all to emerge from the school years feeling hopeful about their futures. A manageable mortgage might just allow you to downshift your career in your 60s to a calmer pace that leaves you more energy and time for family and community.

Living below your means is not about denial. Spending smart today buys you freedom tomorrow—freedom from worry and fear of how you can afford to live the life you deserve.

Buying a Home
First-Time Homebuyer: Can You Afford It?
Buying a home is likely the biggest financial transaction you will ever make. And the prospect of owning a home of your own—a place for you, your family, your forever memories—is so compelling. I get that, but please, listen to me here: Take the time to make sure that buying a home is a financially smart move for you.

Is the Timing Right?

	YES	NO
Do you plan to stay in a home for at least five to seven years?		
Do you have an eight-month emergency savings fund?		
Can you make a down payment of at least 10 percent?		
Is your FICO credit score 720 or higher?		

If you answered yes to all four questions, you have made it past the first test.

If you answered no to any of these questions, I want you to slow down and keep renting. Please embrace your patience as an act of kindness to yourself.

What often gets overlooked in the excitement of buying is the eventual cost of selling. If you intend to sell a home a few years after buying, you could end up losing money on your investment. When you sell, you will owe your agent a commission (typically 5 to 6 percent), and you will have other expenses that can bring your total selling costs to around 8 to 10 percent of the sale price. If you buy today and sell in a few years, you may not have a big enough gain on the sale to cover those costs.

Having an emergency fund and being able to make a solid down payment are a signal you are ready to take on the financial responsibility of homeownership. And having ample savings is also going to help you qualify for a better mortgage when you are ready to buy.

Mortgage lenders check your FICO credit scores to determine if they want to offer you a loan and which interest rate and other fees they might charge you. (FICO scores range from 300 to 850. My online personal finance course, which you can access for free, includes a quick lesson in how credit scores work.) The best mortgage deals are reserved for borrowers with FICO scores of at least 740. You want to get as close to that level as possible. If your score is below 700–720, my advice is to work on getting your score higher before you think about buying a home.

Factor in the Total Cost of Homeownership

I am all for homeownership, if it makes financial sense. But I am always concerned when I hear people say they want to stop "throwing money away" on rent. I usually get some version of "Instead of paying a landlord $1,800 a month, I am going to pay $1,800 in a mortgage and own the home."

That's missing a very important point.

Quick Quiz: To Rent or to Own?

> Sophia and her husband currently pay $1,800 in monthly rent. They are ready to buy a home, but they don't want their monthly housing costs to increase. What base mortgage amount can they afford?
>
> A) $1,800 a month. That's what they currently pay in rent, so no problem!
>
> B) $2,000 a month. After tax breaks, their after-tax cost will be $1,800.
>
> C) $1,300 a month, to leave them more money to cover other costs of ownership.
>
> Correct answer: C.

If that's a shock to you, well, good! I'd rather shock you before you commit yourself to a way-too-expensive home. Not understanding all the add-on costs of homeownership is one of the biggest oversights first-timers often make. Here's what you need to add to your base mortgage amount:

Homeowner's insurance
Property taxes
Utilities
Maintenance

My advice is to increase the base mortgage amount by 30 percent to account for all these costs. For Sophia and her husband, that would mean keeping their base monthly mortgage in the vicinity of $1,300 a month, leaving them $500 to cover all their other costs.

What about tax breaks for homeownership? Well, as of 2018, federal tax breaks have been significantly cut back. The incentive to deduct the interest part of your mortgage payment has been reduced, as has the ability to deduct property tax and state income tax. The net effect is that homeowners in states with high property tax and income tax rates will be more limited in the tax deductions they can claim. That effectively increases the cost of homeownership. I have always advised people not to use the after-tax cost of homeownership as a basis for setting their housing budget. It was always a tip-off that someone was about to overextend. The new tax rules make my advice even more important to consider.

Tune Out What the Pros Say You Can Afford
Mortgage lenders will approve you for the maximum loan amount based on their analysis of your income, other debts, and investments and savings.

I want you to ignore what you are told. Yes, ignore. Here's what a lender won't ask you:

Do you want to help pay for your kid's college education?

Do you dream of retiring at 60 rather than 70?

Do you expect you might at some point need to provide financial support to your parents or loved ones?

A lender is solely focused on your ability to repay a mortgage. The lender does not care whether the mortgage will eat up so much of your cash flow that you will be hard-pressed to focus on other goals.

Here's how to start thinking about your housing budget: How little can we spend to meet our needs?

My challenge for house hunters is to redefine their dream house, reimagine the American dream.

The perfect home is an affordable home.

A fancier house does not buy you what matters. It is the memories you create inside that house—your relationships, meaningful experiences, the love and care that you bring to everyday tasks—that will make your house treasured. Those memories don't have to be in a house that breaks the bank.

Consider a 15-Year Mortgage

The standard mortgage term is for 30 years. My best advice is to make the trade-offs necessary to be able to afford a 15-year mortgage. Because you pay off the mortgage in half the time with a 15-year loan, the monthly mortgage cost will—no surprise—be a lot higher. But the payoff can be a tremendous lift to long-term security. You are out of debt faster, and you will end up paying tens of thousands of dollars less in interest on the mortgage, in part because the interest rate on a shorter term loan is lower than for a 30-year loan.

For a $200,000 mortgage:

> Monthly cost with a 30-year mortgage: $1,015
> Monthly cost with a 15-year mortgage: $1,450
> (Assumes a 4 percent interest rate for the 30-year mortgage and 3.5 percent interest rate for the 15-year mortgage)

But let's look at the bigger, longer-term picture:

Total interest costs on $200,000 mortgage:

> 30-year mortgage: $145,000
> 15-year mortgage: $57, 000

Not only will the 15-year mortgage save you a lot in total interest charges, it is a fantastic way to build financial security. For young homebuyers, you could be mortgage-free before your kids (even those yet to be born) are ready for college. For older buyers, a 15-year can make it possible to be mortgage-free before you retire. As I explain on page 137, I think a key to feeling safe and secure in retirement is not having to worry about a mortgage payment.

My advice, before you start house shopping, is to play around with an online mortgage calculator to see which size mortgage you can afford with a 15-year payback period. For instance, instead of borrowing $200,000 for 30 years, borrowing $150,000 for 15 years would keep your monthly payment in line with the 30-year, but save you plenty in interest charges and build your security in double time.

Remember my advice to live below your means but within your needs? Even if a lender says you can afford the $200,000 mortgage, I want you to slow down and ask yourself: *What would I gain if I bought a less-expensive home that I could pay off faster?*

If a 15-year mortgage is not feasible, make it a goal to pay off your 30-year mortgage ahead of schedule. Making one additional payment a year will shave years off the time it takes to repay the loan. There are free online calculators that will show you how adding to your principal payment will speed up your payback.

Buying a Car

Whenever I meet someone who tells me, wistfully, she wishes she could save more in a Roth IRA, or save up enough to make a solid down payment on a home, I immediately ask what's parked in her garage or driveway.

Typically, it's a car that was bought with a loan that carries a monthly cost of more than $400 a month. Households with two car payments can be spending more on what's inside their garage than the mortgage cost for the entire house.

I have to tell you, the money you spend on cars drives me crazy! You are missing out on a fantastic opportunity to free up money for the financial goals that are important to you. If you spent the least amount possible on cars, imagine what you could do with all that extra monthly cash.

Can we agree that a less-expensive car will certainly get the job done?

A less-expensive car will idle in traffic just as well as an expensive car.

A less-expensive car will get the kids to soccer practice on time and will have plenty of safety features.

A less-expensive car can hold just as much after a Costco or Sam's Club run as an expensive car.

Let's consider two car-buying scenarios:

> Option 1: Spend $450 a month on a car payment.
>
> Option 2: Spend $200 on a car payment. And invest $250 a month in a Roth IRA.

After five years . . .

> Option 1 leaves you with a car that you can keep driving.
>
> Option 2 leaves you with a car you can drive and more than $17,000 in a Roth IRA, if we assume your retirement account grows at an annualized 5 percent.

Even if you stopped saving more in the Roth but let it just keep growing for another 20 years, the $17,000 would be worth more than $45,000. All because you made the choice to drive a less-expensive car 25 years earlier.

And that plays out with every car you buy. Over your lifetime it's reasonable to assume that being a smart car buyer could generate $150,000 in savings. Just imagine the financial security you could achieve with that $150,000.

Your Car-Buying Guide

DO NOT LEASE

Leasing is a big mistake that can keep you in a forever loop of owing monthly payments. A standard car loan is for a set period of time. You make monthly payments for three, four, five or more years. Once you have paid off the loan, you own the car outright. If you bought a new car and paid it off in four years, that could easily give you another five to ten years or so of driving the car—without owing a loan payment. Those are years in which you will have more monthly cash flow to put toward other goals.

With a lease, your payments likely never stop. A lease is typically for 36 months, after which you either can buy the car or take out a new lease. Most people who lease opt for the latter. Thus, they never have any time when they are not making a car payment.

AIM FOR A 36-MONTH OR 48-MONTH CAR LOAN

As I write this, the average car loan is for about 70 months, and one-third of loans are for more than six years. That is not my definition of *smart*.

The average loan term has nearly doubled over the past generation as a way for the auto industry to sell a too-expensive car to households who, through no fault of their own, have seen their incomes stuck in neutral for years. Stretching out loan payments over five or six years brings your monthly payment lower. That's a tempting sales hook. But it is just a ruse to get you to spend more money on a purchase that is guaranteed to lose value.

It's important to understand that a car is a depreciating

asset. That means it loses value from day one. When you sell or trade in your car, you will never sell it for anywhere near what you paid. I get that you will require a car loan, but it makes no sense to borrow more than you need to for a purchase that will only lose value and eventually have to be replaced.

That's why I want you to take out a loan that will be paid off in 36 months, or 48 months at the most. Will that require you to buy a less-expensive car? Yes! That's borrowing smart. Spend less on a car today and get it paid off faster, and you have extra dollars to put toward other financial goals.

Below are some estimates of how much you could borrow if your goal is to get a loan paid off in four years or less. A down payment and trade-in of a current car will add to the total sticker price you can reasonably afford.

	$250 monthly payment		$300 monthly payment		$350 monthly payment	
	36mo	48mo	36mo	48mo	36mo	48mo
4%	<$10,000	<$12,500	<$12,000	<$15,000	<$13,300	<$17,000
5%	<$10,000	<$12,300	<$11,500	<$14,400	<$13,100	<$16,600
6%	< $8,500	<$10,500	<$10,000	<$12,500	<$11,500	$14,750

CONSIDER A USED CAR

There are safe, reliable new cars that cost $15,000 to $20,000. If you have the need for a new-car smell and decide to borrow smart, you can stick with new.

But before you buy new, I'd encourage you to check out the used car market, especially certified pre-owned cars backed by a dealer warranty. One of the best ways to borrow smart is to buy a car that is a few years old. New cars lose about 20 percent of their value after one year. At the end of three years, their value is nearly 40 percent lower. Buy a car that is a few years old, and the sticker price will be 20 percent to 40 percent less than if you bought new.

Now, of course, the used car has some wear and tear. But thanks to manufacturing advances, cars are so much more reliable than they were when I started driving, ahem, fifty years ago. A two- or three-year-old car that hasn't put on a ton of miles can keep running reliably for another seven to ten years, or more.

KEEP DRIVING THE CAR AS LONG AS POSSIBLE

Your goal should be to drive your car for as long as it is reliable. Yet what I see happening is that after three, four, or five years, you come up with some rationalization that you need or deserve a new car. You spend so much time commuting, you deserve to have a nice car. Or you feel like buying a home is out of your reach, so hey, why not buy a nice car. It's still a fraction of what a house costs.

I hope that by now you can understand the huge opportunity cost of that sort of thinking. If you keep a car for five, ten years after you have paid off the loan, those are years where you can tackle other money goals.

How Your Car Buying Can Build Financial Security

	$300 monthly payment for 48 months	$300 monthly payment for 72 months
Payment in month 49	$0	$300
Savings from redirecting $300 payment to savings in months 49–72	$6,900	$0
Continuing to save $300 a month from months 73–120 months.	$14,100	$14,100
TOTAL POTENTIAL SAVINGS IN KEEPING A CAR 10 YEARS	$21,000	$14,100

As I stated earlier, there is a lot of potential money parked in your garage or driveway. Spending the lowest amount possible on a car and then keeping it for as long as possible will give you tens of thousands of dollars (especially if you are a two-car household).

My advice is that the minute you make your last car loan payment, open a new savings account at the bank where you have a checking account. It can take less than five minutes to do this online. Then set up an automatic monthly transfer from your checking account into this new savings account for the exact amount of your old car payment. If your bank or credit union allows you to name the account, give it an empowering name: CarSmart. BigTimeSavings.

You and I both know you can afford to do this. You are just continuing a monthly payment you've been making for years. It is up to you how you want to use this money. Just promise yourself that it will only be used to buy you freedom from worry. Maybe that's making a quarterly transfer into your emergency savings fund. Maybe it's extra quarterly investment in your Roth IRA. Or maybe it's a side fund that will help you help your parents as they age.

College

This is the trickiest financial challenge you will ever face. There is no greater impulse than to provide for your children.

But the system is set up to lead you straight into financial mistakes that can take decades to undo. Parents are allowed to—often encouraged to—borrow as much as they need, regardless of whether they can afford to pay it back. The federal PLUS loan program that provides loans to parents to pay for a child's college costs does not apply the standard vetting lenders use to review car and home loan applications.

No one calculates whether you have sufficient income to handle all your debt payments. No one is checking your credit scores to see if there might be a tip-off that your family is already financially stressed. No one is asking whether you will be able to handle the payments and keep saving for your own retirement. All you need to prove is that you aren't behind on debt payments and you haven't declared bankruptcy recently, and you can borrow through the federal PLUS loan program. Regardless of whether it will put your family's finances at great risk.

This section of The Financial Empowerment Plan, more than any other, will determine the ability of your entire family to thrive in the coming decades. Follow my advice, and you and your children will come out of the college years in great financial shape. That sets you up for a happier retirement. And it launches your children into adulthood with confidence and excitement about their future. Spending smart on college can be the most liberating blessing for your family.

Ensure That You Will Not Be a Financial Burden on Your Children

Okay, I know that sounds a bit crazy. What does it have to do with college financing?

Everything.

We get so caught up in the here and now of our lives, it becomes hard, if not impossible, to anticipate the repercussions of the choices we make today. That can lead us to make decisions right now that can seem so right, so loving, so parental, but that ultimately will cause family heartache down the line.

> I can best help you see this by asking you to check any of the statements below that apply to you:
>
> ☐ I/We are on track with our retirement savings. We are very confident we will be in great shape when we retire.
> ☐ If I/we decided to take out loans for college, we would still be able to continue saving for retirement.
> ☐ I/We work in a field where we see solid job security throughout our 50s and into our 60s. We expect (not just hope) we can continue to work in our careers throughout our child's college years.
> ☐ I/We do not carry credit card balances.
> ☐ I/We are prepared to step in and provide financial support to our own parents if the need arises.

Unless you confidently checked every box, I need you to understand that borrowing for college could cause your kids incredible heartache.

Let's flash forward a decade or two after your child is done with college. You are approaching retirement age; maybe there are grandchildren beginning to arrive. What should be a wonderful stage for your entire family is, sadly, draped with anxiety.

Because you borrowed so much for your child's education, you can't afford to retire. Either because you still have those loans to pay off, or the borrowing you did caused you to stop adding to your retirement funds during the kids' college years. So now when you run the retirement calculators, you are concerned about what you see.

You are game for working longer, to keep bringing in income and tucking a little away for your retirement years, yet you worry whether your employer will let you keep working.

That's a recipe for a multigenerational financial mess. If you ultimately do not save enough for retirement, your kids will need to step in and provide financial support. Maybe you have done this for your parents, or you watched your parents do it for your grandparents. It is always done with love and with no regrets. There is no fiercer act of love than to take care of family. But that does not mean it comes without great cost.

Please know that I am not just talking about the impact on the family's finances. There's an emotional cost that comes with having to stretch your spending today to support loved ones, knowing that it will likely cause the cycle to repeat with your own children. That's a dynamic that causes multigenerational stress. I am asking you to consider what it will take to break that cycle.

I know you do not want to impose that on your children. I know you do not anticipate that will be the case. But I ask you to seriously review the questions I asked above. They are the questions that, if answered honestly, will reduce the chances of your putting your children in the position of needing to help support you.

If borrowing for college will put your family at future financial risk, I ask you to stand in that truth. Not borrowing for college can be the most powerful and loving gesture you will ever make.

Worried about disappointing your kids? Here's what I hear from so many young adults in their 20s and 30s: They are shocked and guilt-ridden when they finally figure out what their parents did to pay for college and how that has put their parents' future at risk. They tell me they wish they had known at 17 what they know at 27 and 37. They would have gladly made different college choices if they had known the impact it could have on their parents' future.

Do your kids right: Be honest about your ability to borrow.

Have the Talk in Ninth Grade

Every family needs a college financial game plan. The goal is to have a variety of schools to choose from that will not break the bank. But to have that flexibility in the spring of your child's junior year of high school requires advance planning.

Starting in ninth grade, begin to think about building a list of potential schools that fall into three buckets:

1. Dream schools. These are the schools at the top of your child's list, but you will ultimately consider them only if the aid package will allow your family to emerge from school with a manageable level of debt. (We will discuss that in a bit.)

2. Great schools that will offer more aid. Starting to plan in freshman year in high school gives you time to work with counselors and do research to find schools where your child may be such a catch that she will qualify for a generous aid package. (And by aid, I mean grants and scholarships. As I explain in the next step, many schools disguise parental loans as aid. You are not going to fall blindly into that trap.) I think of these as financial dream schools: places your child will thrive at, but that also are truly, honestly affordable.

3. In-state schools. I don't need to explain that a state school will cost one-third or less what a private four-year college might cost. A state school can deliver a great education at the right price. (I also recommend considering community college as a smart path for your family. There are plenty of careers that require a two-year associate's degree. Or you and your child can hatch a plan to start at a community college and then transfer to finish at a four-year college. That can greatly reduce the cost of college.)

The goal is for your child to apply to schools from all three buckets. If the dream school comes through with a great aid package, you're set. But if the dream school is going to make a financial mess of your family's future, I want you to have better, smarter options.

UNDERSTAND THE DIFFERENCE BETWEEN AID AND LOANS

When your child is accepted at a school and you have applied for financial assistance, you will be presented with a financial aid award letter.

There is no uniform standard for how these letters must present the package. The sad fact is that schools routinely consider loans as "aid."

It is up to you to carefully review the award letter to understand the costs the school is absorbing in scholarships and grants, and the costs they expect you to pay for through loans that you and your child take out.

Take Out Federal Loans, Not Private Loans

There are two types of college loans, federal loans and private loans.

> **Federal loans:** Available through the government. Families must complete the Free Application for Federal Student Aid (FAFSA) to be eligible. The federal Stafford loan is not need-based; any student can borrow. The interest rate is fixed; it will never change. The federal PLUS loan is for parents to borrow for a child's education. It is also a fixed-rate loan, and there are no income limits. Federal Perkins loans are reserved for students who have exceptional financial need.
>
> **Private loans:** Available from banks, credit unions, and online lenders. Eligibility and terms are based on a financial analysis and credit check. Private loans can be fixed rate or variable rate.

Your family should use only federal loans. Private loans are dangerous. They work a lot like credit cards. Most private student loans have variable interest rates. The rate can rise when general interest rates increase. And as with a credit card, if you trip up and miss a payment, the lender can raise your rate.

Federal loans charge a fixed—permanent—interest rate. Federal loans also offer a lot more flexibility in repayment. There are a variety of different payback plans, even loan forgiveness if you work in certain public service fields. None of that is available with private loans.

Kids Borrow First: Federal Stafford Loans

I know you wish you could provide everything for your child. But please remember what we discussed earlier: Your family needs to make smart decisions today that will help all of you feel secure tomorrow.

And having your kids borrow first is the smartest college financing move. The interest rates on federal student loans are much lower than the interest rate charged on federal PLUS loans for parents.

Federal Stafford loans are available to all students, regardless of family income. Please read that again: Every student is eligible for a federal Stafford loan. If you need to borrow, and your family is not eligible for a Perkins loan, a Stafford should be your first option.

Here's what I like about federal Stafford loans:

You can't really over-borrow. There are annual loan limits. In 2018 the limit is $5,500 a year for freshmen, $6,500 a year for sophomores, and $7,500 for juniors and seniors. Children who are not claimed as a dependent on a parent's tax return can borrow more.

A terrific rule of thumb is that a child's total college borrowing should not exceed what she can expect to earn in her first year out of school. College aid expert Mark Kantrowitz says that if you follow this guideline, it's likely the child will be able to handle a standard 10-year repayment plan, which is exactly what you want.

A reasonable interest rate. Stafford loans charge a fixed interest rate. The rate is set each summer and uses a formula that is tied to the interest rate on a 10-year U.S. Treasury note. For the 2017–2018 academic year, the Stafford loan rate for undergraduates was 4.45 percent. Families that meet certain requirements may qualify to have a portion of their Stafford loan "subsidized." This means that while the student is in school, the government pays the interest due on the loan. Unsubsidized Stafford loans require the student to be responsible for the interest while in school. (Most students opt to have the in-school interest charges added to their loan balance rather than pay the interest while in school.)

Flexible repayment programs. While it is best to aim to repay a loan within 10 years, the federal loan program also has options that can spread the payment out over a longer period, or be pegged to your income, as a way to help you handle the payments. You may also be able to qualify for loan forgiveness after 10 years if you work in certain public service fields.

Providing Parental Aid

I meant what I said above. If taking out a loan to help pay for your child's education means you will need to scale back your retirement saving or makes you have to work well into your 70s, that's not acceptable.

But I realize some of you may be in a position where you can borrow a responsible amount. Here's how to proceed, carefully:

Borrow via the federal PLUS loan program. The interest rate is fixed. The rate for the 2017–2018 academic year was 7 percent.

If you have a terrific FICO score of at least 740, you may be able to qualify for a private student loan with a lower rate. Please be very careful. If the rate is adjustable, your borrowing costs could rise. And keep in mind that if you die and still owe money on a private loan, the lender will expect your estate to keep paying. With a federal loan, the debt dies with you.

Aim to repay the loan in 10 years or before you retire (whichever is sooner).

The standard repayment period is 10 years, though there are options to take longer. Needing longer than 10 years is a sure sign you are borrowing too much.

At the website BigFuture, which is run by the College Board (bigfuture.collegeboard.org/pay-for-college/loans/parent-loan-repayment), you can calculate what your monthly payments will be. For instance, borrowing $25,000 a year for four years works out to a monthly payment of around $1,200 for 10 years, assuming a 7 percent interest rate.

Again, no one is going to tell you that it is too much. You have to stand tall and make a responsible choice.

A responsible choice means knowing that even if you did not receive another raise for 10 years, you could handle the payment. Even better, given the iffiness of staying employed throughout your 50s and 60s, would you be able to handle the payback if you were laid off and your next job paid 10 percent less?

III. BUILD YOUR FUTURE

I know that for many of you, the topic of retirement planning triggers anxiety. Given what's at stake, given all the moving pieces, I absolutely understand that response.

But here is what I need you to know, right here and now: You have everything it takes to flip the switch from anxious to confident.

You do not need to find any new superpowers to tackle retirement planning. There is no advanced financial math you need to master. Nor do you need to become an investing expert if you don't want to. All that is needed is that you summon the nurturing, kind, and supportive qualities you bring to others—at home, at work—and focus that energy on your future.

Retirement planning is a 360-degree win. It's an act of generosity that will radiate in all directions. Removing the anxiety creates more space for happiness today. That, in turn, enriches the quality of your relationships, both personal and professional. And knowing you are doing what is within your control to build a secure tomorrow is going to blanket you in newfound peace.

The first step is to take a few deep breaths. On each exhalation speak these words of truth to yourself:

Fear comes from inaction. I am ready to remove worry and anxiety from my todays by making smart and strong decisions that will build retirement security.

Across the Generations

I recognize that one of the big obstacles is being, justifiably, overwhelmed by all that falls under the heading of Retirement Planning. And those online calculators that say you need to save a gazillion dollars to retire aren't just demotivating, they are terrifying.

I hear you. I feel the anxiety.

I have a plan.

Actually, I have two plans:

> "Retirement Planning Before Age 50" begins on page 120.
>
> "Retirement Planning for Those Who Are 50+" begins on page 130.

What a young and fabulous 27-year-old daughter needs to focus on is different than what I want her mother (or grandmother or aunt) to tackle.

That said, I'd love for everyone to read both sections. To learn. And to help each other.

Retirement planning is the most devilish of financial goals. It is 100 percent dependent on mastering delayed gratification. Every smart move is about making a choice today that will benefit you decades later. There's no immediate payoff. Dieting for two months is hard. And here I am asking you to stick to a retirement plan for the rest of your life.

Not exactly easy, or natural.

That's where community can be so important. We can encourage, cajole, commiserate with one another. We support each other in so many ways. There's not a relationship we won't talk about—spouses, lovers, colleagues, bosses, siblings, kids, kids, kids. Talking helps us work things out; it offers us support and perspective. We all have people we turn to for their wisdom.

Yet money is a walled-off topic that is not discussed.

By isolating money, we give it more power to gnaw at us. Retirement planning is a lifelong process. Rather than tackle it in isolation, I encourage you to draw your girlfriends, family, colleagues, and friends close, and make it another part of your sharing circles. For support. For motivation. For the calming perspective that comes when we realize we are not alone.

LET'S KEEP TALKING. . . .

Becoming a smart, secure, and strong woman in control of her money is a process. As you embark on your personal journey I hope you will join in and share your experiences, questions, triumphs, and frustrations with other women. I host a weekly *Women & Money* podcast. And I am so excited that we are building an online community for *Women & Money* where you can share, help, encourage, and get your questions answered. Go to suzeorman .com/women to learn more.

My Promise: A Very Focused Plan You Can Achieve

I could fill a book or two with retirement planning advice (and I have!). But I also know that too much information or a too-long To Do List may backfire. Presented with so many tasks, you may never find the will to get started, or you might quickly lose your motivation.

I have taken all that to heart and honed my advice to focus on the absolute essentials. In each of the two plans, there are four main steps I want you to tackle. Four. Not fourteen. Not forty-four.

Follow through on the four steps, and you will have taken a massive leap forward in building retirement security. If in the process of following my streamlined retirement plan you find yourself interested and motivated to learn more, that's great. Not necessary, but great! My online Personal Finance Course that you can access for free at SuzeU.com/activate (use the activation code MONEY) includes more detailed information on retirement planning.

But I want to be very clear: Every woman who completes my four-step plan is doing a fantastic job. You are controlling the biggest, most important factors that will give you confidence today, and you are taking control of building a secure tomorrow.

Advice Across the Ages: A Quick Spin Through Retirement Accounts

Before we dive into the specific plans, I want to share some basic information that is important to understand.

SPECIAL ACCOUNTS FOR RETIREMENT

There are two types of investment accounts specifically for retirement savings.

Workplace retirement plans. Some of you may have the opportunity to save for retirement through a workplace plan such as a 401(k) or 403(b). In 2018, anyone younger than 50 can contribute up to $18,500. The annual limit is $24,500 if you are at least 50 years old.

Many workplace retirement plans offer a "matching contribution." If you agree to save some of your salary, your employer will kick in a contribution as well. For example, a common matching formula is for an employer to match 50 percent of a worker's contribution up to 6 percent of their salary. That means that if the worker contributes 6 percent, the employer will deposit another 3 percent into her account. That's a deal no one should ever pass up.

Contributions you make to a workplace plan are automatically taken out of every paycheck and invested in your retirement account. That's a great way to stay committed to saving.

Individual retirement plans (IRAs). These are accounts anyone can open at a low-cost investment brokerage such as TD Ameritrade, Schwab, Fidelity, or Vanguard. In 2018, anyone younger than age 50 can invest $5,500 annually. The limit is $6,500 for anyone at least 50 years old.

The best way to invest in an IRA is to arrange a direct deposit from your checking account into your IRA account. This will take less than 10 minutes of your time to set up online at the investment firm where you have your IRA. Then you can have money transferred biweekly, monthly, or quarterly. You set the frequency. What's important is that you automate the process.

To save $5,500 a year (the 2018 IRA limit for anyone younger than 50):

• Set up 26 biweekly transfers of $211.
• Set up 12 monthly transfers of $458.
• Set up 4 quarterly transfers of $1,375.

To save $6,500 a year (the 2018 limit for anyone at least 50 years old):

• Set up 26 biweekly transfers of $250.
• Set up 12 monthly transfers of $541.
• Set up 4 quarterly transfers of $1,625.

There are two distinct styles of 401(k)s and IRAs you can choose between: traditional accounts or Roth accounts. Whenever you have the option to save for retirement in a Roth 401(k) or Roth IRA, grab it!

The main difference in these accounts is the timing of when you pay your IRS tax bill. With Roths, you essentially pay your tax bill today—your investment will come out of income that has already been taxed—and then in retirement, you can use money in your Roth without owing any tax. With a traditional account, you get a tax break today—your investment is made with income that has not been taxed, which reduces your current tax bill— and then in retirement every penny you withdraw from your traditional account will be taxed as ordinary income.

I strongly recommend you always choose the Roth 401(k) or Roth IRA when you have the option. Tax-free income in retirement is going to be so very valuable.

Retirement Planning Before Age 50
Step 1: Save at Least 10 Percent of Your Salary

What you manage to save is 100 percent in your control. How your savings grow over time, based on the performance of stock and bond markets your retirement accounts are invested in, is not in your control.

Yet so many people make the mistake of focusing all their time and energy on how their money is invested when their future depends more on how much they manage to save each year. If you are saving too little, how that money is invested won't make up for your too-low savings rate. Even worse, it can lead you to be too aggressive with your investing when you realize years from now that you don't have enough saved for retirement and you want to try and catch up by making riskier investments.

Your Retirement Goal: I want every woman—every household—to aim to put at least 10 percent of their salary into retirement savings each year.

Notice I said "at least" 10 percent. Saving 15 percent of your pretax salary in a retirement account is my best advice, but I don't want to scare you off. Get to a 10 percent savings rate ASAP. That's a fantastic step. My hope is that you will be so energized by that accomplishment, you will then keep pushing on to get to a 15 percent savings rate.

> Multiply your annual pretax salary: $_____ x 0.10
> = __ (your annual retirement savings goal)
> Divide your annual retirement savings goal by 52:
> = $_____ (your weekly commitment to your future)
> Plug your weekly savings goal into your new declaration of retirement security:

"Saving $_____ a week is my commitment to giving myself the future I deserve. What I save today is not a sacrifice. It is a blessing that I can banish the fear and worry that comes from doing nothing."

Why am I telling you to save so much?

You could spend more than two decades in retirement. It is no longer rare to live until age 90. The safe-not-sorry assumption financial advisors use when building retirement plans for clients is to assume living until age 95. Think about that: If you retire at 65, your savings need to help support you for 30 years!

You shouldn't count on the markets to do the heavy lifting. One of the big mistakes I see is that people assume their retirement accounts will grow at 10 percent or so, on average, each year. That's way too optimistic if you ask me. Successful retirement planning is not about hoping for the best. You want to make conservative assumptions to ensure you will be fine even if the markets don't deliver knockout returns.

Throughout the plan, you will see that I use a 5 percent rate of return in my assumptions. That's half the long-term historic rate of return for stocks. That's not me being overly cautious. It's me giving you the highest probability of success. If your retirement plan is based on a conservative rate of return, you can be more optimistic that you will reach your goals. I am also giving you some breathing room. If returns are in fact higher, you may be able to scale back your savings in your 50s if your accounts have grown bigger than anticipated. That can be an incredible advantage and is far better than hitting your 50s only to find that your accounts are nowhere near where they need to be to give you a secure retirement.

Step 2: Getting Started: Choose the Right Type of Account

ALWAYS GRAB A MATCHING CONTRIBUTION

> Q: Do you have a retirement plan at work that offers a matching contribution?
>
> ☐ **Yes**
>
> ☐ **No**
>
> If **No:** Go to the next section on Roth IRAs.
>
> If **Yes:** Always contribute enough to your workplace plan to earn the maximum company-matching contribution. Once you reach that amount, you should do more retirement savings in a Roth IRA.

About six in ten workplace plans offer both a traditional account or a Roth account. (And more add this option each year.) As I mentioned earlier, please choose the Roth account. Because you are only going to invest in the company plan up to the point of the match, you will also want to save in a Roth IRA.

For those of you who were "automatically enrolled" in your workplace plan, you may in fact be saving in a traditional account. That's the default your employer may have chosen for you. Contact the plan and switch over to the Roth account for your future contributions.

SAVE IN A ROTH IRA

> Q: If you are single, is your modified adjusted gross income (MAGI) below $120,000? If you are married and you file a joint federal tax return, is your

modified gross income below $189,000? (MAGI is a mouthful, but for most of you it is very close to the adjusted gross income you reported on your federal tax return.)

☐ **Yes**

☐ **No**

If **Yes:** You are eligible to invest the full $5,500 (in 2018) in a Roth IRA account. You may also be able to make a smaller contribution if you are single and your MAGI falls between $120,000 and $135,000, or if you are married and your MAGI is between $189,000 and $199,000. (These levels are adjusted periodically for inflation.)

If **No:** Invest in a traditional IRA. Given your high income, it is unlikely you will qualify for an upfront deduction on the amount you contribute. But the traditional IRA is still worth it, as your money will not be taxed during the decades it grows. That's called tax deferral, and it is a valuable tool to build retirement security.

A SPECIAL NOTE TO STAY-AT-HOME PARENTS AND NONWORKING SPOUSES

Just because you don't earn a paycheck doesn't mean you can't have a Roth. You can have a spousal IRA, be it a Roth or a traditional. The money you invest in the IRA can come from the income your spouse earns. But what I especially like is that the actual account will be in your name only—not in your spouse's name and not held as a joint account. That's a nice power move. In reality, if you were ever to divorce, money acquired and invested during a marriage is going to have to be equitably distributed. And in community property states, it typically is an automatic 50-50 split. But having the account in your name puts some control and responsibility in your lap— and your lap only.

Once you've maxed out on the matching contribution and/or your IRA, you can keep saving more. I hope you do. Here's your strategy:

If you have a workplace plan: Remember, the first step was to only invest in a workplace plan up to the point of earning the maximum match. Now you can increase your contribution rate. Or, if there was no match and you started with a Roth IRA, now you can add savings in your workplace plan.

If you max out on an IRA and don't have a workplace plan: Open a regular account at the same brokerage firm. There is no limit on how much you can save in a regular account. (For guidance on how to invest in these accounts, see chapter 7, "Bonus Section: Investing on Your Own.")

Okay, you now have the foundation for saving for retirement.

Start with a 401(k) or 403(b) if there is a match. Set your contribution rate high enough to get the maximum match. But no higher. Choose the Roth version if it is offered.

If you don't have a workplace plan, or there is no match, start your saving in a Roth IRA.

Ready to save more than the IRA max? Contribute more to a workplace plan, or save in a regular taxable plan.

Step 3: Invest for the Long Term

Now we need to talk about how you will invest the money you are contributing to a workplace retirement plan and/or an IRA. Your retirement accounts are like an empty suitcase. It is up to you to decide what goes inside of them: stocks, bonds, cash.

STOCK UP

When you have decades to go until retirement, my advice is that the majority of your retirement accounts should be invested in stocks because over time, stocks provide the best chance of earning returns that will help your accounts grow at a pace enabling you to afford your life 40 or 50 years from now.

The reality of investing is that stocks will periodically go through bad stretches—called bear markets. But through the years they have always recovered and go on to reach new highs. And you have plenty of time to wait for the recoveries.

That said, during stock bear markets, U.S. government bonds tend to hold up quite well when stocks falter. Owning a small portion of bonds can provide some strength to your portfolio when stocks are weak.

RECOMMENDED STOCK/BOND MIX WHEN
YOU ARE YOUNGER THAN 50:

- **85 percent:** Stocks (60 percent U.S. and 15 percent international stocks)
- **15 percent:** Short or intermediate-term bonds
  There are many free online asset allocation tools you can use to figure out the right mix for you.

Invest in the lowest-cost mutual funds and exchange-traded funds.

Mutual funds and exchange-traded funds (ETFs) offer an easy and affordable way to build a retirement portfolio that owns hundreds, even thousands, of individual stocks and bonds. That's how you achieve *diversification,* which is just the fancy-pants term for not putting all your eggs in one basket.

You only have to make one investment—in the fund or ETF—and you become an owner in all the stocks and bonds it owns.

401(k)s. You are limited to the investments offered by your workplace retirement plan. Typically, these are mutual funds.

IRAs. You can choose among all the funds and ETFs offered by the firm where you have your account. My recommendation is to always seek out the lowest-cost index funds or ETFs.

Every fund and ETF charges an annual fee called the expense ratio. Your goal is to pay the smallest ER possible. The less you pay, the more of your money stays invested for your retirement. There is no reason to pay an expense ratio of more than 0.50 percent for an index fund or ETF. In fact, many terrific options charge less than 0.20 percent. It is easy to find the ER listed online, or you can call customer service and ask.

STRESSED OUT? OPT FOR A TARGET RETIREMENT FUND TO GET STARTED

You can build a diversified portfolio with as little as three different index funds/ETFs. I think that's the best way to go. However, if the thought of having to make investment decisions seems a bit daunting or just too big a time imposition at this juncture, I hear you.

A target retirement fund, often called target-date fund or (TDF), can take all the heavy lifting off your To Do List. A TDF automatically holds (and adjusts over time) the proper types of investments—according to investment pros—based on how many years you have until retirement. For example, if you pick a target fund with a retirement date forty years off, it will start out owning mostly stocks; then, as you get closer to retirement, it will automatically scale back its investments in stocks and shift to less risky investments. The fund will also automatically "allocate" your investments in a wide range of types of stocks: stocks from different countries, stocks from different industries, small stocks, large stocks, and so on.

All you need to do is choose a TDF with a date that is near the time you expect to retire. For instance, if you are 30 years old, you might look for a TDF with the year 2050 or 2055 in its name.

Most workplace retirement plans offer target retirement funds. The majority of younger people saving in workplace plans opt for them. And all the big investment brokerages you can choose for your IRA also offer target retirement funds as an option.

DON'T BE SCARED BY BEARS

Once you start investing for retirement, your biggest challenge will be to stay invested when the markets get scary. When a bear market hits, our brains start working overtime screaming at us: *Sell, sell, sell.*

If you think like that, you've got it all wrong. When you are young, bear markets can actually work to your favor if you keep investing. As stock prices fall, the money you continue to save from your paycheck or through an automatic deposit into your IRA account will buy more shares. For instance, if you invest $400 a month and the share price of a mutual fund is $40, you can buy 10 shares. If the share price falls to $24, your $400 will buy you 16.6 shares. Because you have decades to go, owning more shares today is what you want. Let's say that 20 years after the bear market, the share price is now $65. Ten shares would be worth $650. If you kept buying during the bear market, your 16.6 shares would be worth nearly $1,100.

Tempted to sell anyway and then jump back in when the worst is over? Well, as reasonable as that sounds, it is very hard to pull off with any success. There's no big announcement or clarion bell that proclaims, "Hey, the bear is over. It's safe to dive back in." Investors who sold typically find it hard to decide when to return to investing in stocks. Sitting in cash and missing bull markets is not going to get you to your retirement goals.

Step 4: Hands Off . . . Until You Retire

Money you are saving for retirement needs to stay invested for your retirement. Unless you have an absolutely dire emergency—out-of-pocket medical expenses you can't cover through other savings or your income—you are never to raid your retirement accounts.

It is very important to resist the temptation to "cash out" your workplace retirement account when you leave a job. There is a huge opportunity cost if you pull money out of your retirement account today:

A WITHDRAWAL TODAY OF . . .	. . . IS STEALING THIS MUCH FROM YOUR FUTURE RETIREMENT:	
	25 years	45 years
$5,000	$17,000	$45,000
$20,000	$68,000	$180,000
$50,000	$169,000	$449,000

Assumes 5 percent annualized rate of return

Once you take the amazing step of saving for your future, please don't undermine yourself by making an early withdrawal. Your future self will be so very grateful you kept the money working for your best interests.

When you do leave a job, I recommend doing what is called an IRA rollover, which moves the money from your old employer's retirement fund into an IRA account you have set up at a brokerage or fund company. Once your money is in an IRA, you have more investment options; if you can lower your investing costs with a rollover, that is the way to go. You can learn more in my online Personal Finance Course. (Go to SuzeU.com/activate and use the activation code MONEY.)

Retirement Planning for Those Who Are 50+

I know you are still very much in your prime, but your early 50s is the perfect time to give your retirement plan a thorough checkup. Do that now, and you are giving yourself 15 or 20 years to make smart, strong, strategic moves that will help you land at retirement in solid shape. Wait until you are 60 or 65 to see where you are, and you leave yourself little time or room to adjust.

Step 1: Get an Estimate of Your Annual Income in Retirement

How much you have saved up is not a very helpful number. What you really want to know is how much annual income that number can generate for you in retirement, without running out too fast. The trick with your retirement funds is that you don't want to withdraw too much in the early years of retirement and then run the risk of not having money to support an extra-long life.

The good news is that it's now a fairly easy task to figure out how much monthly or annual retirement income you are on pace to have. Your workplace plan, or the company where you have your IRAs, should have a free online calculator that will give you a personalized retirement income estimate based on your savings, estimated Social Security benefit, and any other income sources. Or you can use the free online AARP Retirement Calculator.

I hope what you find out is that you are on track. But if the estimate of your monthly retirement income came up short of what you had hoped, please don't panic. We still have 15 to 20 years to get you in even better shape to enjoy the retirement you deserve. Please focus on what is possible from this day forward. Now might be a good time to circle back to what I asked you to embrace at the beginning of this retirement section:

Fear comes from inaction. I am ready to remove worry and anxiety from my todays by making smart and strong decisions that will build retirement security.

One option at this juncture is to increase what you are contributing to your retirement plans.

Remember, once you are 50, the annual contribution limits are higher for 401(k)s and IRAs. In 2018 you can save as much as $24,500 in a 401(k) and $6,500 in an IRA.

There is so much you can achieve in the next 15 years (or more). I offer you this moment of savings motivation:

The 15-Year Sprint to the Finish

Saving this much more a month	can increase your savings by
$100	$27,000
$400	$107,000
$1,000	$267,000

Assumes 5 percent annualized rate of return

There is one caveat to consider. If you are determined to stay in your home when you retire and will not have the mortgage paid off, I explain in Step 2 (see page 135) that you may want to consider paying off your mortgage rather than turbo-saving more in your retirement plans.

Can't imagine how to save another penny more? On to the next step.

SAVE MORE BY SPENDING LESS

It is the rare household that has no give in its budget to squeeze out more money for retirement savings. It is also the rare household that thinks this is true.

For decades, I have counseled individuals and families who come to me with a shortfall problem. They can't pay their credit card off each month. There's not enough to build an emergency fund, there's no way they can afford the premium for term life insurance.

They want to take control of their financial life, but they tell me they just don't make enough money. That's usually not the entire problem. Lifestyle creep is a part of their problem. Even for people who understand the difference between needs and wants, the needs end up being way too expensive. Yes, you need a car, but you could have bought a much less expensive one. Yes, the kids need clothes, but they do not need the pricey jeans they ask for yet you can't seem to say no to.

This sort of lifestyle creep can build up over time. You struggled as a 20-something, but as your career and income grew over the past few decades, so too have your spending habits.

If the retirement income estimate you got in Step 1

wasn't what you had hoped for, scaling back on spending today is how you can help your future self. Not just by freeing up some money that can be saved in retirement accounts. One of the most overlooked benefits of cinching in your spending a notch or two today is that you are also recalibrating your future retirement income needs. Living on less today means needing to generate less income in retirement to maintain that lifestyle.

NIP AND TUCK

Let's start with the low-hanging fruit in your monthly spending.

I am a big fan of finding small spending trims that, when added together, can add up to $100 or $200 more a month in savings. That is then $100 or $200 more you can devote to retirement savings.

Drop down a tier on the cable and cellphone plan. Extend the number of weeks between cuts and mani/pedis. Stay in one more Saturday night a month. I bet you can find $1,000 in savings a year that can be redirected into retirement savings. Probably more.

Yep, those are all lifestyle choices I am asking you to consider trimming. If you insist on being a glass-half-empty-type person, you are likely feeling dejected right now that I am asking you to rein in your lifestyle.

Once again, I ask you to open your head and heart to an alternative interpretation. It's not about going without less today; you are giving yourself more for your tomorrows. How is that not empowering? How is that not a reasonable trade-off to consider?

Women & Money readers can access my online Expense

Tracker, for free. It's a great tool for helping you recognize where you can trim spending so you can save more. Go to suzeorman.com/women and use the activation code WOMEN.

CARS AND COLLEGE: YOUR SOURCE OF RETIREMENT SECURITY

As I explained in the Spend Smart section of The Financial Empowerment Plan, there is a tremendous amount of future security that can be wrung out from not overspending today on big-ticket items.

If you happened to glide past that part of the FEP, please circle back. Taking that advice to heart is how you can unearth big sums of future retirement security.

For instance, drive the cars you have, longer. Every month you keep a car after paying off the loan is a month where you have more money to put toward retirement. And when you do need to buy a new car, buy the cheapest car possible. Your car strategy can generate $200 or more a month in savings for long stretches that can be redirected into your retirement accounts.

And those of you with children who will be college-bound in the next 15 years, you must open your heart and head to the advice I shared in the previous section. As counterintuitive as it may seem, as emotionally challenging as I know it is, focusing on saving for your retirement rather than paying for college is the most loving step you can take. It will help you remain independent as you age, rather than needing your adult children to step in with financial aid for your retirement. That's the gift for your adult kids. And in the here and now, if you follow my college spending advice, they can still have a great education that is affordable.

Step 2: Home In on Retirement Security

Most 50-somethings these days report that they intend to stay in their home rather than downsize or move to a less-expensive neighborhood or region. Or the tendency is not to think about it all right now; you'll wait to see how you feel at 65 and make some decisions then.

I am asking you to do some serious thinking right now. The questions you should be asking yourself today:

- **If you intend to move between now and retirement, would moving sooner than later free up sizable savings?**

I know this is a big ask. It's your home, not your car, I am suggesting you sell. But if you take the time to step through the payoff, I think you may find it easier to make your move today. The financial weight that can be lifted can make all the difference today *and* in retirement.

If you are currently paying a mortgage, could you sell your home and buy another home mortgage-free? Or if your intention is to rent, how much lower could your monthly rent be compared to the mortgage, property tax, and maintenance costs you have as a homeowner?

    A: Your current monthly housing costs: $ _____
    B: An estimate of downsized monthly housing
       costs: $ _____
    C: Subtract B from A: $ _____ (your estimated monthly
       savings)

What could that monthly savings buy you? Maybe more money to save in your 401(k) or IRA. Maybe the money to have a wonderful restorative vacation each year that you pay off in full. Far from an indulgence, recharging your batteries is how you can help yourself work longer—a popular retirement strategy we will discuss in the next step—rather than burn out earlier.

- **If you intend to stay put, have you honestly run the numbers to make sure you can afford the property tax and maintenance?**

Now that you have the monthly retirement income estimate from Step 1, will there be enough to easily handle these fixed costs? If it's a stretch today, it's likely going to be a challenge in retirement.

- **Will your home be comfortable for an older you?**

The home that worked so well to raise your family, the home that is full of memories, is not necessarily the perfect home in retirement. How many stairs are there to navigate into the home, up to the bedroom? Is there a bathroom near the master bedroom where the door opening is wide enough to accommodate a walker? Is the laundry inconveniently located in the basement? I understand those questions may make you feel a bit uneasy, but that's nothing compared to how uncomfortable you will be in retirement if you find yourself stuck in a home that isn't kind to an older you.

Many near retirees are tackling renovation projects today to make their home more hospitable for their retirement years: building a master suite on the first floor, revamping the bathroom to have the space to maneuver with a walker, and maybe installing a walk-in shower.

If you want to remodel your home for your retirement years, I am again going to ask you to spend smart. Can you honestly afford the renovations? If you intend to use a home equity line of credit or home equity loan to pay for the work, your borrowing should be limited to what you can afford to pay back within five to seven years, or before you retire, whichever comes sooner.

- **Will you have the mortgage paid off before you retire?**

I am concerned that the answer many of you just gave was no. The percentage of homeowners at least 65 years old who still had a mortgage climbed from 22 percent in 2001 to 30 percent in 2013, and I have every reason to expect the trend to continue. Many of you bought a new home between 2000 and 2007 and refinanced during the past decade when rates were so low. That could leave you with 20 or more years of mortgage payments.

If your intention is to stay in the home when you retire—and you are confident you can afford to pay the ongoing taxes and maintenance costs—you must make it a goal to pay off the mortgage before you retire. There is no greater pressure release valve than to be rid of a mortgage payment when you begin living off of your retirement income.

While today's younger adults have the chance to do all of their retirement saving in Roth accounts, it's likely that much, if not all, of your retirement savings is in traditional 401(k)s and IRAs. And that can create a bigger hurdle in retirement if you intend to still have a mortgage.

Remember, every dollar you withdraw from a traditional retirement account will be taxed as ordinary income.

So let's say you have a $1,500 a month mortgage payment. That's $18,000 a year you need to pay the mortgage. That's going to require withdrawing a lot more than $18,000. You would need to withdraw around $25,000 a year to be left with the $18,000 you need, after paying your federal (and state, where applicable) tax.

That can put a lot of pressure on your retirement savings. Not only do you not want to deplete your savings too fast in retirement, but also, the larger your withdrawals, the bigger the tax bill you may face, because all of your withdrawals will be counted as taxable income. Moreover, the amount your Social Security benefit is subject to income tax, as well as your Medicare Part B and prescription drug coverage premiums, is based on how much taxable income you have. The higher your income, the more those benefits can cost you.

Now that you understand why I am so eager for you to pay off your mortgage before you retire—assuming it is your forever home—here's how to do it: Contact your lender or loan servicer and ask for an updated "amortization schedule" that will have your mortgage paid off by the time you are 65.

Even if you intend to keep working past age 65, I still want you to aim to be mortgage-free by 65. You can't control your health; working longer may not be practical. Or you may find yourself pushed out of a job sooner than anticipated.

Consider saving less in your retirement accounts so you can get the mortgage paid off.

Yes, you read that correctly. I am telling you to save less

if it frees up the cash you need to get the mortgage paid off before you retire.

Ideally you can ramp up your mortgage payments today by tightening your spending a bit to find the extra cash. But if that's not going to do the trick, you can temporarily ratchet down your retirement savings contributions.

If you have a workplace retirement plan that offers a matching contribution, you must continue to contribute enough to earn the maximum matching contribution from your employer. There is never any circumstance where I would advise you to pass up that match.

But beyond that base savings, I have no problem if you reduce your contributions if it helps you find the cash to get your mortgage paid off before you retire.

Step 3: Work on a Working-Longer Plan

Working longer can indeed be a great tool for building retirement security. Not only does it give you more time to potentially save more, it reduces the number of years you will live off of your retirement savings.

I am a big believer that everyone should consider 70 the new normal retirement age. If you can afford to retire sooner, that's great. But I think planning to age 70 is practical and responsible. With the likelihood you could live into your 90s, retiring at 62 or 65 puts too much pressure on many retirement savings accounts. That's a lot of years to support yourself!

But having the intention to delay the date you retire can be an extremely dangerous strategy if you don't carefully plan. I am all for your 50-something self's having the intention today that you will keep working until age 70. But intentions aren't guarantees.

Many people who expected to keep working into their late 60s find themselves retiring sooner than expected. Due to a personal illness. Due to caring for someone with an illness. Due to burnout. Due to being pushed out ever so deftly by management that is careful not to make it about your age. (As if!)

This is where you need to plan, not just hope.

Stay cutting edge at work. The skills that got you to your current status as a respected 50-something employee or business owner will not necessarily sustain you for another 15 or 20 years. You must commit yourself to having every skill that a 25-year-old new hire brings to the table.

Yet what I see happen so often is that older workers don't keep current. They invest all their energy into hoping they will somehow be able to have an extended run. That might work when the economy is humming, but you better realize that at the first whiff of an economic slowdown, employers will start the cost cutting. Employees with outdated skills will be the first targets.

If you are lucky enough to have on-the-job continuing ed, you are nuts if you don't reserve a seat at every session or devour every online offering. And take a hard look at where the business seems to be headed—are there new skills and jobs that are in demand? Talk to your manager and HR about the skills they are hungry to see over the next few years. Then get to work on making yourself a valued employee for the future by going back to school. There are plenty of free and affordable online courses. Or check out the curriculum at local community colleges.

Plan a smooth segue to a post-career job. The reality is that you may not need—or want—to stay in your current career job throughout your 60s. Or it may not be practical; look around your current office. How many 60-somethings are there?

Downshifting to a less demanding (lower-paying) job can be all that is needed in your 60s. You can give your retirement plan a big shot in the arm simply by not tapping your savings in your 60s or not taking a reduced Social Security benefit in your early 60s. (More on this in the next step.) And all you need to pull that off is to make enough money to pay your living costs. If you can't keep contributing to your retirement savings, that's okay. You are still helping yourself plenty by making enough money so you can delay touching any of your retirement savings for a few more years.

Maybe you cover your living expenses by taking on consulting work. Or projects. Or maybe it's your chance to follow a less-lucrative passion, whether it is a hobby you want to earn some income from, or maybe giving back by teaching or coaching.

The point is, you need to plan for your 60s' work life. Will you need to take some courses to get a certification? Or maybe you need to double down now on networking and starting to consult on projects. That will be a lot better than trying to make the shift cold turkey once you leave your career job.

Step 4: Plan for Your 90-Year-Old Self (95 Is Even Better!)

Once you turn 65, I have news for you. You need to appreciate how young you really are.

QUICK QUIZ

> If you are 65 in 2018 and in average health and you aren't a smoker, what are the odds that you may still be alive at age 90?
>
> A. 17 percent
> B. 31 percent
> C. 46 percent
>
> Answer: C. There's a near 50 percent chance you will still be alive at age 90. That's not exactly an outlier possibility. A 65-year-old woman in excellent health has a 54 percent probability of still being alive at age 90.

I hope that delivers some valuable perspective. Please don't fall into the trap of thinking the day you retire is some sort of end date or a countdown of sorts. Your 65-year-old self could be very alive for another 30 years. She's got a lot of living left to do. And that requires some careful planning.

KEEP INVESTING FOR SOME GROWTH

You may stop working full-time at 65 or 70, but don't assume your money can stop working hard. You certainly want to invest more conservatively than you did in your 30s and 40s. But that doesn't mean all your money belongs in cash or bonds.

One of the big challenges in retirement is to invest in a way that keeps your portfolio rising—over time—at a rate that is at least in line with the annual increase in living costs. Your grocery bill, health care costs, and housing expenses 20 and 30 years from now will be more than today. The rising cost of goods and services is called inflation. The long-term annual inflation rate is around 3 percent. So you want your investments to earn at least that much. As I write this, cash accounts earn just 1 percent or so. And most high-quality bonds have yields (interest payments) of less than 3 percent.

Keeping a portion of your investments in stocks gives you the ability to earn higher, inflation-beating returns over the long term.

How much? Well, a pretty good rule of thumb is to subtract your age from 100 (or 110 if you want your plan to assume you will live to 95). The result is how much you might want to keep in stocks. A 65-year-old might have 35 percent invested in stocks, a 70-year-old, 30 percent.

Get the biggest check possible from Social Security. Once you turn 62, you have a great opportunity to boost your retirement income with one simple but often hard decision: Do not begin your Social Security retirement payments.

Yes, age 62 is when you are allowed to take Social Security retirement benefits. But if you start at 62, you will be accepting a lower payment than if you wait.

There are three key claiming milestones:

> **Age 62.** You are eligible to start taking your retirement benefit. Claim at age 62 and your benefit will be up to 30 percent less than if you wait four or five more years.
>
> **Normal retirement age.** This is the year when

you are entitled to 100 percent of your earned benefit. Your normal retirement age (also called full retirement age) is somewhere between 66 and 67 based on the year you were born.

Age 70. This is the starting age that will qualify you for the largest possible benefit. For someone with a normal retirement age of 67, waiting until age 70 will entitle you to a monthly payment that is 24 percent higher than if you started at age 67. There is no investment in the world that can deliver a guaranteed 24 percent gain over three years.

Might you die before age 70 or before you collect enough payments to "break even"? Yep. Yet that's so not the point. Anyone who makes those arguments isn't focused on what really matters: providing security for the possibility you will still be very much alive through your 80s and into your 90s. Delaying until age 70 essentially "buys" you more retirement income for your later life. While you may ponder the prospect of dying, I am focusing on how very long you may live and giving you a way to have the highest possible income in your 80s and 90s.

Please consider delaying taking Social Security until you are 70. You can tap your other retirement income sources, such as your 401(k) and IRAs, while still letting your Social Security benefit grow to age 70.

SOCIAL SECURITY FOR MARRIED COUPLES

Ladies, please read this very carefully. Widows are entitled to one Social Security benefit. When a spouse dies, the survivor can choose to keep her benefit or switch over to the benefit of her deceased spouse. You don't get to collect both. Just one.

The smartest move, the crucial move I strongly encourage every married couple to consider, is that the spouse with the highest earnings delay starting Social Security until age 70. That's how you can ensure that whoever is the surviving spouse will be able to collect the highest possible benefit. It does not matter who is older. All that you need to focus on is having the spouse who's the higher earner delay.

If the other spouse wants to start collecting before age 70, that's okay, though that partner should please try and wait until normal retirement age.

You can get an estimate of your expected Social Security benefit at different claiming ages at the Social Security website (ssa.gov). Search for "Social Security Estimator."

CONSIDER LONG-TERM-CARE INSURANCE

Anyone already in her 50s doesn't need to be told that getting old can be a health challenge that carries a great financial burden. Whether you yourself have helped your parents navigate older age or you've been the shoulder a friend leaned on as she cared for elderly relatives, you likely understand what's at stake.

One of the most profound and liberating steps you can take when you hit 50 is to buy yourself some financial insurance to help if you become unable to fully navigate your day-to-day life on your own.

Long-term care insurance (LTCi) can provide the money to hire someone to help you with these activities, or to pay for care in an assisted living facility or nursing home.

The fact that women live longer than men increases the likelihood that we may at some point be widowed and unable to care for ourselves. A sobering reality of aging is that one day we may no longer be the wonder women we once were, caring for our parents, our children, our husbands, our friends. One day we may not even be able to care for ourselves. Whether it be at-home care or care in an assisted living facility, we may indeed need help. A few of us will need nursing home care. All of it is expensive. A health insurance policy will not cover this kind of care. Nor will Medicare. So who will pay for long-term care if it's needed? You will—out of your own pocket. Caring for your latter-life self is the biggest threat to your retirement savings. If you need lots of support, you run the risk of outliving your savings. When you have spent most of your money, Medicaid will pay, but you won't have as many choices.

That's why I ask every woman to carefully consider long-term care insurance once she turns 50. An LTCi policy can provide the money to hire someone for additional help at home, or you can use LTCi to help pay for nursing home care, if it is ever needed.

Why my insistence on tackling this project when you are just 50 years young? Because if you decide LTCi makes sense for you and your household, it is smarter to buy it when you are younger and healthier than to try to obtain coverage a decade from now when preexisting conditions can make you ineligible, or a policy too expensive.

And to be very clear: If you are married or living with a life partner, I want you both to consider LTCi. There is no more physically and emotionally demanding job than being the primary caregiver to an ailing spouse.

LTCI BUYING TIPS

Unfortunately, buying LTCi insurance is not as easy and straightforward as buying term life insurance. It is not exactly cheap; an annual premium can be anywhere from $2,000 to $3,000 or more. And insurers can get approval from state insurance commissioners to increase the premium costs for existing policyholders. When that happens, the increases can be 30 percent to 50 percent or more.

Doesn't exactly sound like a great sales pitch, does it? I am in no way pleased that to date the industry has done a lousy job of figuring out how to correctly price these policies. That said, it is likely that these growing pains, for what is a relatively new type of insurance, will not continue at the same pace for anyone buying a policy today. The LTCi industry is now using better assumptions that should reduce the need for major premium hikes going forward.

And I think that even with the premium challenge, LTCi is still very much worth considering. Just take a step back and focus on the bigger picture: If you ever need care, your premiums will be a small fraction of the benefits you can tap.

I am recommending that you carefully think through whether a plan makes sense for your household. The AARP has a solid primer on LTCi considerations (search for "AARP Understanding Long-Term Care Insurance"). And

I have learned so much from LTCi expert Phyllis Shelton, whose consumer website (gotltci.com) is a good place to start your learning.

Among the key factors I want you to consider:

Buy a policy you could still afford if the premium doubled. I don't want you to ever feel a policy has become so expensive that you let it lapse. That's such a tragic waste of all the years of premiums you paid. It is far better to buy a scaled-back policy today that you will still be able to afford if sometime in the future you are hit with premium increases.

Involve the family. I respect that $2,000 to $3,000 (or more) a year is a lot of money. But it is an expense I bet your adult kids will be very eager to help you with. Don't give me the pride side-eye. This is how you protect your kids: If they are able to chip in to help you afford a solid LTCi policy, you have just helped them out of a potentially huge crunch years from now. Without an LTCi policy, they may find it necessary to help pay for your care later on, or curtail their careers to step into the full-time caregiver role.

Grab the inflation rider. One way insurance agents can lower the premium cost if there is sticker shock is to offer a policy that does not provide an inflation adjustment. I recommend you always purchase a policy with this insurance protection. I would rather you reduce other benefits—if necessary—such as purchasing a policy with a lower lifetime benefit than forgo this important protection against ever-rising care costs.

Be kind to your future self with a healthier attitude today. Lifestyle choices you make today can play a role in how seamlessly you transition to retirement. I am not going to tell you how to exercise or what to eat. But I am going to cheerlead. Your body and your mind are your two most valuable assets. Invest in them and the payoff can be enormous. You are bound to feel better today and potentially help yourself land in retirement in better shape, and happier. Being able to enjoy your retirement strikes me as the ultimate goal of retirement planning.

IV. GIVE TO OTHERS

Family Finances

You don't exist in this world alone. You are at the center of a web of relationships, and navigating them can be very complicated, especially when money is involved. The vast majority of women I meet have problems not with money per se, but with relationships. The money problem is usually a symptom or a consequence of the relationship problem. In previous chapters, we talked about how women equate giving with a show of love, so when we love a person or a cause so much, our nurturing soul directs us to give, give, give. We give money, even if it means digging into home equity lines of credit, ringing up more debt on credit cards, or cosigning loans. We say yes to whatever is asked of us, rather than stopping to assess the impact it will have on our lives emotionally and financially. We tend to let other people set the agenda for us. They tell us what they need, and we put their needs front and center, even if it means sweeping everything *we* need aside. We are more committed to helping others than we are to helping ourselves.

Are you one of these women?

- The woman who knows deep down that an emergency savings account is the core of financial security, but when her sister falls behind on the mortgage, car, and credit card payment for the umpteenth time, she once again cleans out her only savings account because she can't imagine not helping.
- The wife who knows deep down that the equity she and her husband have in their home is an asset that should be saved and protected, not spent, but when her husband has his midlife crisis and announces that he wants to quit his job to pursue a start-up business, she doesn't have the heart—or courage—to say no.
- The woman who knows deep down that her best friend is a financial train wreck but still agrees to cosign a car loan for her, which means most likely she will end up paying for that friend's car, even though she cannot afford to do so.
- The daughter who sends $500 a month to her parents to help them with their bills, even though that means she doesn't have the money to cover her own expenses.
- The stay-at-home mom who is in charge of the household shopping and bill paying, but can't make ends meet on what is in the bank account and assumes it is her fault.
- The bride-to-be who is too afraid to ask for a prenuptial agreement or talk about money before her wedding date because she thinks it will take the romance out of the relationship.
- The beloved employee who kicks in $25 every time she is

asked to contribute to a co-worker's wedding present, birthday party, or Christmas celebration, even though it puts her behind in paying her own bills.
• The mother who continues to bail out her adult children from their mistakes.

What I find both moving and encouraging is that women who find themselves in these kinds of situations realize, on some level, that they are just as much the problem as those who are making the money demands on their life. Loving someone you are committed to does not mean that you always have to give money; it simply means you have to be able to give of yourself. And giving of yourself takes us right back to the eight qualities of a wealthy woman, for it takes more power to say no out of love than to say yes out of weakness. I want you to consider this concept for another moment because it's a big one, ladies. It takes more power to say no out of love than to say yes out of weakness. This notion is at the very heart of establishing a healthy relationship with your money.

This section of The Financial Empowerment Plan is all about helping you learn how to engage with your family from a position of love. What I want more than anything is for you to experience the calm and confidence that comes when you know your choices are nurturing everyone. Everyone! Including you!

If you have read this far, the notion of being generous to yourself should not be an uncomfortable jolt. You now know that putting yourself first is anything but selfish. It is the singular act that will enable you to care for and support your family in a manner that uplifts you all. It is only when you are strong and confident that you are in position to give the very best of yourself to the relationships that mean everything to you.

Be as Committed to Yourself as You Are to Others

As straightforward and logical as it may seem to talk to those you love from a place of power and honesty, in reality it is probably one of the hardest things you will ever have to do. Saying no to someone you love is difficult. It is easier to make a mess of our finances by saying yes all the time than to live with the fear of what the word *no* will do to our relationships. But as every woman who has fallen into this habit will tell you in hindsight, making money decisions in the hope of saving a relationship always backfires. That is why we go right back to the mainstay of keeping you in a healthy relationship with your money. Are you doing what is easy, or are you doing what is right?

Write it. Read It. Live It.

I love my smartphone and all my tech, but I also still lean on some low-tech ways to motivate. The simple act of writing down an intention and putting it in plain sight—not buried in an app that I have to remember to open—can be incredibly helpful and powerful.

EXERCISE: GET IT RIGHT

Pull out a piece of paper (a Post-it is great) and a pen.

Write these words: **From this moment on, when it comes to my money and my relationships, I promise always to do what is right rather than what is easy.**

Sign and date this intention.

Place it where you will see it repeatedly. A bathroom mirror. Your laptop case or the corner of your desktop. The car dashboard.

Every time you see it, repeat the truth at least three times.

My hope is that by constantly connecting to this thought, it becomes a guiding principle throughout your day. Before making any moves with money—your own money or money that you share with someone—I want you to ask yourself, **Am I doing this because it's the right thing to do or because it's easy?**

It's easy to tell your boyfriend you'll lend him money that you don't have. It's easy to give your kids money even if it comes from your emergency fund. It's easy to avoid the topic of a will or trust with your husband because he's afraid of his own mortality. But doing what is easy is not how you build a healthy relationship—with people or with money.

Establish a Collaborative Process for Handling Money Decisions with Your Honey

It's so easy to hand over responsibility for financial matters to your partner. For those of you married to a man, history works in favor of that, as handling the money was always viewed as the man's domain. But it's the twenty-first century, my dear ladies. It's time to let go of that dynamic. I see far too many women of all sexual orientations lazily let their spouse or partner handle the money stuff because it mystifies them or doesn't interest them. Being in control of your financial destiny requires that you be an active participant—not just by paying bills, but in overseeing your investments, too. Take this step, and I think you will be surprised how it will give you confidence that will radiate throughout your life and help your relationship.

I have a funny story to tell you. When I decided to write this book, I began my research and sought out experts and professionals who specialized in working with women. After speaking to many of them, I decided it was time I stopped asking questions in general about women and started asking personal questions about how the women experts themselves handled their money. The answers I got startled me, to say the least. One brilliant academic admitted that her life partner handled their finances—she just didn't want to deal with them; she tried to read the statements, but none of it made any sense to her. Besides, she trusted him to take care of everything.

"So let me get this straight," I said. "I have just been on the phone with you for over an hour and you can tell me every hormonal, biochemical, and psychological reason why women behave in certain ways, yet you don't feel you have what it takes to understand money?" Well, you can imagine that she got a (compassionate) earful from me. To repay the favor of the time she spent on the phone with me, I offered to review all her financial statements to make sure that her partner knew what he was doing with their money.

The next morning, she sent me one statement after another, along with a note explaining that after our conversation, the professor couldn't stop thinking about what I had said to her about being in control of her own money. And that night at her request, her partner walked her through every financial statement and explained everything to her. He was thrilled, finally, to have her involvement, and she was so happy, too, because for the first time she really understood what was going on in her financial life. Her partner had, in fact, done a great job with her money, so I called to tell her that. When she picked up the phone, she told me she felt like she had a healthier relationship—with her money and her man. He actually loved and respected her more for taking this step. She also confessed that their sex had never been better—if only she'd known, she'd have gotten involved with her money sooner. (See what I mean about people telling me everything?)

I also see women failing to step into the money conversation in new relationships. No matter if you are 22 and about to share a studio apartment, or 52 and about to share the beautiful home that you own outright, you must talk money before anyone moves anywhere. How will you split the rent or the mortgage payment? The grocery bill? What if he or she makes three times the amount you do?

Depending on where you are in your relationship, here's how to make sure you and your honey are doing what is right, not just what is easy:

When a Newer Relationship Gets Serious

In my perfect world, all couples would be open about their finances from the get-go. I am well aware this is not how it often plays out. Money is the last thing anyone wants to talk about. But you are absolutely nuts if you don't start talking, and planning, at the point you consider moving in together.

The number one stressor in relationships is money. So

often the problem is framed as arguments over not having enough money. I think that misses the real underlying missed opportunity: having a united vision and plan for how you will handle money issues. You can have plenty of money, but if you and your partner are not in sync on how to spend, save, and share that money, your relationship is going to be severely stressed.

You are not going to fall into that trap.

Share your FICO credit scores. I have to tell you, this is the quickest and most revealing window into the financial makeup of your life-partner-to-be. I know this isn't going to win me any romance awards, but I firmly believe that any person who is financially irresponsible is more likely to be emotionally irresponsible in a relationship. For that matter, if you are the one with a messy credit history, you owe it to your potential life partner to come clean. Now, if you or your life partner has a low FICO score, the relationship isn't doomed. I am in no way saying a FICO score below 740 is the new relationship litmus test. The point is that you must both be honest and open about your financial situation. Ultimately you should support each other in terms of stepping forward and fixing whatever financial mistakes you have made in the past. Lasting love and commitment is dependent on how we get through the messy stuff in life. But when the mess is so deep and ingrained, you also need to have the courage to exit a relationship—not only because it will financially drain you, but because it is so emotionally costly. Sharing your FICO scores is an important conversation starter.

Moving In Together? Preplan How You Will Cover Shared Expenses

I know your biggest concern is how you will split the closet space, but what should really be at the top of your list is how you will split the bills. Too often I hear of couples who move in together and then discover they had completely different assumptions about how they would share the finances. Assuming is not the way to go. Before anyone makes a move, make sure you agree on how the bills will be split. Do not automatically take for granted that 50–50 is the right answer. What if you make $100,000 and your partner makes $50,000? Is it fair to split everything 50–50?

Split Decision: A Formula for Determining Who Pays What

A. Your monthly take-home pay: $ _____ + your partner's take-home pay: $ _____ = _____ total household income

B. Add up your shared monthly housing expenses: $ _____

C. Divide your total monthly expenses (B) by your combined take-home pay (A): = _____%.

The percent in C is what you will each contribute to cover your shared expenses.

Your monthly take-home pay x C = $ _____ your contribution to household expenses

Your partner's monthly take-home pay x C = $ _____ your partner's contribution to household expenses

An example: Let's say your after-tax pay is $7,000 a month, and your love brings home $3,000 a month. Your total household after-tax income is $10,000. Now add up all the expenses you have each month that keep the household running. Let's say those expenses for utilities, rent, phone, and so on, come to $3,000 a month. Divide $3,000, your joint expenses, by $10,000, your joint take-home income, and that will give you 30 percent. That means that you each have to put up 30 percent of your take-home pay toward expenses, or $2,100 from you and $900 from your love—equal percentages, not equal amounts.

Set up a joint checking account to pay for household bills. Yes, keep your own checking account, but set up one together. (I also highly recommend that you set up auto-payment for your household expenses.) This is a great testing ground for your money habits. One week before your appointed bill paying, both of you are to have deposited your share of the monthly expenses into that account. There are to be no slipups and no excuses. As far as I am concerned, this is a litmus test to see how financially responsible your love interest is, and for your love interest to gauge the same about you.

Before You Marry

Given that women on average are marrying/partnering for the first time later in life, chances are that when you do find the right person, you may already have a lot of financial baggage in the form of assets and debts. And so, too, may your fiancé or life partner. The basic rule is that you are jointly entitled to assets accrued during a marriage, and you are both on the hook for debts accrued during the marriage. Anything you bring into the marriage is not automatically shared. Yet I have seen so many women run into trouble by switching titles or not clearly spelling out what is theirs—and not ours.

I've taken a strong position on this for a long time: I believe in prenuptial agreements. It has never been more important given the career success so many women bring into their relationships. If you are remarrying, this becomes even more important. I am not suggesting that either of you hoard what is yours, but with so much on the line, I want you to state clearly to each other what you expect to remain separately owned and what you expect to become shared assets or property.

Fine-Tune the Money Decisions in a Long-Term Relationship
Many of you who have been married or partnered up for years may not have the healthiest financial relationship with your honey. For a number of you, the problem is that you have let your partner handle most of the decisions. At some point you may have been so grateful that you didn't have to "deal" with it all. But now, not so much. You realize it has created an odd imbalance in your relationship. Or perhaps you have watched a friend, or mother, or sister struggle to get her financial bearings after a divorce or becoming widowed. Or maybe it's what you have learned while reading this book that brings you to a new place: You want to be more involved with the money decisions. You are hungry for the emotional payoff that will come when you make sure you are taking care of all the financial matters that are within your control.

I am thrilled if you are ready to make this shift. I hope your partner is just as thrilled. But I ask you to be patient and respectful in how you convey this change to your partner. You are pulling up a chair to join your partner at the table, not to take over. You want to be working together, side by side, building your financial security.

Here's how you both can navigate your way to a healthy financial relationship:

Create an accusation-free zone. Please approach this as a collaborative endeavor. You are not putting your spouse or partner to the test or questioning his or her choices. This is your partner, your lover, your life mate. Respect that bond. If you do find that some decisions that have been made run counter to the advice in The Financial Empowerment Plan, talk it through. No accusations. Others deserve the "no shame, no blame" treatment as much as you do. I hope your spouse or partner is a financial whiz and made all the right moves for your family, but quite often I see women mistake enthusiasm for expertise. If there are some mistakes in your plan, no worries. The point is that you are now a team that can make the necessary financial adjustments.

Now, if you are years into a relationship with someone who actually likes the old-fashioned dynamic of being in total control of the money, you obviously want to be sensitive to that. Take the time to explain that although you are becoming involved with the finances, it is not about your spouse/partner giving up power or you questioning your partner's abilities. It is about your need to be knowledgeable and involved, to share the responsibility for your collective financial future.

Agree that who earns what is irrelevant. When our world seems to increasingly, depressingly equate money with power, I realize it may be a challenge to not let money rule in your household. But I am convinced it's just a natural (misplaced) habit that you and your partner can overcome.

The bottom line is that all money decisions are to be collaborative. The primary breadwinner has no more say or sway over a decision. This is especially important for non-working spouses to embrace. Actually, it is important for every woman to embrace. If you are not earning an income or you earn a fraction of your spouse's income, you must not equate that with being powerless. In a healthy, thriving, loving relationship, a paycheck does not assign power. Any woman who does not embrace this is putting herself seriously on sale.

Do you know how often stay-at-home spouses tell me they don't know how to ask their partner for money to buy something the household needs or—God forbid—something for themselves? Curiously, they tend to be responsible for the monthly bill paying but not the family's long-term investment strategy. The thankless job is theirs, and when there isn't enough money to cover the monthly expenses, they are the ones made to feel guilty. Often the problem is that there simply isn't enough money coming in to cover all the bills, not that the stay-at-home mom isn't financially responsible. But women put up with this dynamic. It's my guess that they have an underlying sense of guilt or gratitude that their spouse is the one working while they get to remain at home. I want every stay-at-home mother today—and those of you who think you may go this route someday—to listen up and listen good:

The job of the stay-at-home parent is equal to the job of the breadwinner.

Please read that again. Your job is as important, as vital, and as necessary as that of the spouse who earns a paycheck. That is just as true for any woman who is not working outside the house, regardless of whether she is raising kids. Money is never to be a power tool wielded by the breadwinner.

No spouse should ever need to ask the other for money or have to ask permission to spend a dime. That is wrong, wrong, wrong. Who earns the money is not the issue. The money that is earned is both of yours. Period.

This spirit is just as important in households where the wife is the main breadwinner, an increasingly common dynamic in many households.

Now, what I've seen happen time and again in this dynamic is that the wife tends to disown her power and downplay her role as breadwinner. She doesn't talk about it; she backs away from any acknowledgment of it because she doesn't want her husband to feel bad or "less than." In fact, this kind of behavior enables the man to create a dysfunctional relationship of his own with money! Many times I've seen men in this situation get themselves in trouble financially. Spending money becomes a matter of pride, and so by whatever means necessary—borrowing against credit cards, taking out a home equity line of credit, whatever it takes—having money to burn like a big shot becomes all-important. (Interestingly, stay-at-home dads don't seem to suffer from this problem. Once a man makes the decision to run the household, that becomes his job; it is his choice to raise kids rather than funds—and therefore easier to reconcile this to himself and others.)

The solution to this problem? Start talking. Understand

that no matter what he says, his thoughts are not in harmony with his words and actions. Let him know he's not the only one who feels uncomfortable; let him know that you're in this together, that you're both blazing a new trail here. Most important, it is critical that you both understand this change won't happen overnight. So keep talking, until his and your thoughts, feelings, words, and actions are in perfect harmony.

Drop the judgment. It saddens me that I still hear from many women that their husband gets annoyed or critical when the monthly bills are higher than he thinks they should be. In far too many households it is the responsibility of the wife to pull the rabbit out of the hat to make ends meet. Please listen to me: When there isn't enough cash to pay for basic living costs, that's a shared problem. It's not your fault. Nor is it your spouse's fault. No more finger-pointing or arguing at the end of the month when the bills are too high. You must create a new dynamic for working together to reduce your money stresses.

I also see tension in households where the basic bills are covered, but the spouses have very different notions of what discretionary spending is okay. You think his penchant for the latest sneaker or tech is frivolous. He's none too thrilled with your overflowing closet. This can be fairly easy to get past if you have more money than you need to cover the essential bills each month. If after paying the bills, funding your retirement accounts, and making sure the emergency fund is topped off at eight months of living costs, there is still money left over, split it 50–50.

And I do mean split it: You both should have separate checking accounts in addition to the joint account that all bills are paid from. The money in your respective checking accounts is a judgment-free zone. You both can spend it (or save it) as you wish, with the full blessings of the other spouse.

You, the Kids, Your Money: How to Help When They Are Young (and Older)

Do you know how many adult children come to me with a mix of anger and sadness about how they feel their parents let them down financially by not being honest? Children who suddenly learn in their twenties and thirties that Mom and Dad don't have any retirement savings because they plowed every penny into their children's college education. Or even worse, they financed college with a home equity line of credit they intended to pay off once the kids were out of school, but then they were suddenly pushed into early retirement and couldn't find a new job at 55. So now the children are worried that Mom and Dad will lose the house if they can't repay the loan, and then where will they live?

I also hear from young adults who find themselves struggling to stay on top of all their bills, especially student loans. Yet for all their years in school, no one taught them how to handle money. I lay a lot of the responsibility on the parents: Before you send your kids out into the world, you need to teach them how to be financially responsible. Here's what it takes:

TEACH THE YOUNG ONES WELL

Be honest—with yourself and with your kids. Being a good parent is not dependent on what you spend on your children. If you do not have the money for the $150 pair of jeans or the latest video game, you must tell them that.

Simply putting it on your credit card is dishonest. It prevents you from moving toward a life in which you are financially secure, and it gives your kids the false impression that they can have whatever they want. That child ends up being miserably in debt as an adult, because he or she knows no better.

And as we discussed in the Spend Smart section of the plan, be honest, too, about paying for your children's college education. As far as I am concerned, there is no more loving gesture you can make to your children than to ensure you will have financial security in retirement. That is your priority. If you simply don't have the money to save for both retirement and their college costs, then retirement must be your focus.

Be a teacher. Our ability to handle money responsibly is not something we are born with. It is something we learn. And unfortunately, our educational system does a lousy job of teaching personal finance to kids; the reality is that it is rarely part of any school curriculum. So the job falls entirely to parents. You must teach and show your kids the value of money.

Once children turn 12 or so, I think it is wise to involve them in the family finances. Have your kids sit with you as you pay the bills—not to make them feel grateful for what you provide, but so they have an understanding of what life costs. Here's an idea: Let your child guess how much the monthly electric bill is. You might find that he or she will think twice before leaving lights or the TV on after leaving the room.

One of the most important lessons you can impart is how to handle credit cards. If you have a strong FICO

166 WOMEN & MONEY

score, I recommend adding your child to an existing account as an "authorized user" when he or she reaches the age of 15. That entitles your child to use the credit card while you get the bill; you then have the opportunity to educate, set limits, and so on. It also entitles your child to start building a credit history based on your FICO score. That can be a huge leg up for your kids once they graduate from college. With a solid FICO credit score, they will have an easier time renting an apartment, and chances are they won't have to make big deposits to open accounts with the gas company, the cellphone provider, etc.

House Rules for Boomerang Kids

More and more households include young adults who never moved out or have returned after college. For many kids, saving money is a primary motivation. Given the high cost of rent in many regions and large college loan balances, this can be a smart move.

But there is to be no free ride.

This is not about you needing your kid to pitch in. The issue is that your kid is now an adult. Time to expect, encourage, and lead them into adult behavior. That's not being mean or cranky. It's loving your kid, by treating them with respect for the adult they are and who they want to become—a thriving, independent person.

Charge rent. How much you charge is up to you. But it must be auto-deposited into your checking account every month on the same day.

Cringing at the thought of doing this? Again, this is about helping your child begin to flex adulting muscles. That's an act of love at this stage of their life.

If you are truly on track with all your financial goals—the eight-month emergency fund is set, your retirement funds are on pace—accept the money as a temporary caretaker. Every month after you are paid, tuck the cash into a separate savings account; you can set up an auto transfer from your checking account into your savings. When your child is ready to move out, you can surprise her by returning the money—or a portion of it. You've just jump-started an emergency fund, or helped with the security deposit, or helped her pay down some more of her student loan debt.

Confirm they are on track with student loan repayment. The worst financial mess your child will ever encounter is falling behind on student loans. There is no escaping this debt; it is rarely discharged in bankruptcy. The best assist you can give your child is to help strategize on how to get the debt paid off ASAP. Ideally, that will be within a standard 10-year repayment window. If your child is moving back in because of student loan debt, please sit down and confirm what the repayment plan is. If you have the financial means to help accelerate their payments, that's a great gift. But I still want you to charge some rent, too. This is Real Life 101 . . . it just happens to be back at home with you.

Insist they save in a Roth IRA. One condition for staying under your roof is that they are not to squander the fantastic opportunity that comes with youth: money they set aside now will have decades to grow. Saving for retirement in your 20s is a huge advantage. If your adult child has a job, I want you to insist they do some saving in a Roth IRA.

Again, you can help here, if you are on pace with all

your financial savings goals. Offer a matching contribution. For every $1 your child saves in the Roth, you will add 25 cents or 50 cents. Or $1. Up to you. The point is you are helping them establish a great habit in their early adult years that will make it so much easier for them to reach their retirement goals.

Have them pay for their health insurance and their portion of shared accounts. Adult children can stay on their parent's health insurance plan until the age of 26. That's fine with me, but if you are paying a premium for your child's coverage, you are to expect your child to reimburse you for this. Again, this is not because you need to, but because you are helping your child learn the way of the world. Same with the cellphone; if they are still on your plan, that's fine. But they need to pay their share of the plan. And if they are web surfing and movie watching on the house Wi-Fi, you better tell me they are contributing to that bill as well.

Recognize That Love Does Not Mean You Must Cosign for Family or Friends

A relationship that is defined by what you put into it materially is not a healthy relationship. Saying it another way: You can be the most supportive and loving parent, friend, sibling, cousin, etc., without ever giving away a penny. Money is not central to any relationship and is not a prerequisite for maintaining a relationship. To think otherwise is to devalue yourself and the relationship—and by now you know you are to never put yourself on sale!

Yet I'm aware that this is another vexing commitment for women. We feel so guilty if we are doing better than a

THE FINANCIAL EMPOWERMENT PLAN 169

financially struggling friend that we agree to cosign a loan or cosign a credit card agreement without weighing the risks to our own financial health. Or when a beloved brother who has already gone through bankruptcy calls to say he needs a $25,000 loan for another ill-fated financial gambit, we say yes, even though the money totally cleans out the cash in our emergency savings account. Or when our cousin calls looking for investors in his new business, we decide to forgo the $5,500 retirement contribution this year so we can help him launch his dream.

And then there's the kids, and maybe the grandkids. You are very proud of them, so when they come to you asking you to cosign on the car loan they can't get on their own, you say "Of course, dear," without considering the financial risk you have just undertaken.

Emotionally, every one of those actions makes perfect sense. But emotion doesn't build financial security. You cannot let your heart dominate every decision in your life. You must engage your head, too. It is a delicate balancing act, but so often I see women just let everything fall onto the emotional side of the scale.

A woman who is in touch with the eight qualities will use them to contemplate the financial impact of always saying yes to friends and family in need. Remember, you never want to give money that depletes your financial security. It's that nurturing trait running amok again, so let me repeat: You cannot give if it weakens you.

I would be doubly cautious of anyone who needs your help in getting a loan. You need to realize that lenders love to give out money; it's how they earn a profit. So if a lender sees something in your friend or brother that makes them nervous enough to insist on a cosigner, you should be nervous, too. Please understand that when you cosign a loan, you are essentially agreeing to pay off the debt. If you are unable to live up to that responsibility, your financial life is going to be a mess.

COSIGNING FOR A GROWN CHILD

I understand the impulse to help, but you need to ask some important questions.

Can you afford to make the payment yourself? If you can't honestly say yes, you have no business agreeing to cosign. Cosigning is a formal commitment that you will make the payments if the borrower doesn't.

Will you ever need to take out your own loan? Once you cosign for a loan or credit card, the loan balance and the payment history will show up on your credit report. If you anticipate you will be borrowing in the future, the existing balance on your cosigned loan could make it harder for you to qualify for the loan you want.

Can your child qualify for a smaller loan without a cosigner? Are you being recruited because your child has his eye on an expensive car rather than a more economical one? Could your daughter buy a house without your help if she lowered her price range? It is not your job to finance what they want; it is your option to help them buy what they need.

Will your child agree to automated payments? In the past, I would insist that any parent who cosigned for a child make the payment directly: The child pays the parent, and then the parent can be assured the payment is made to the lender on time. But with the ease of technology, I am fine if you want to entrust your kid to set up automated payments from her checking account. But she should happily agree to send you confirmation showing the payment posted, each and every month.

COSIGNING SCHOOL LOANS: GETS AN F IN MY BOOK

As I explained in the Spend Smart: College section of The Financial Empowerment Plan, there are two types of college loans, federal loans and private loans. Private loans are dangerous, for many reasons, and my strong advice is to never use them. If that means your child will need to attend a different school, that is the stronger truth to honor. If your child asks you to cosign a student loan, that means it is a private loan. Please don't agree to this.

COSIGNING FOR AN ADULT FRIEND OR RELATIVE

While I understand the impulse to help a child who is just starting out, I am not in favor of cosigning for an older adult. My general advice is never to cosign a loan or a credit card agreement for someone who can't get either one on his or her own. It's a clear sign they have problems being financially responsible. And your commitment to them should not rest on your willingness to be their financial backstop.

I also want you to exercise the same caution with anyone who comes to you for a personal loan. If you must say yes, please treat this for what it really is: a business transaction.

Perhaps the hardest step to take is to gauge whether your financial help really is a supportive gesture. Loaning money to a sister who is knee-deep in debt because her husband refuses to get a job and keeps tapping their home equity is not as kind and generous as it may at first seem. What your sister really needs is your emotional support to stand up to her husband and insist that they no longer pile on more and more debt. Giving her money doesn't change her husband's behavior. In fact, it might just give her an excuse to avoid the problems in her marriage. It might ultimately be more supportive not to lend money—at least until she takes some steps to address the matter that caused the financial mess in the first place.

Helping Your Parents

As your parents age, the contours of your relationship will likely evolve. In addition to the bond of love and support you have always provided, you may also find yourself stepping into the role of financial caregiver. Keeping track of bills and taxes can become tricky as we age, to say nothing of health insurance claims. A recent national survey reports that more than 90 percent of caregivers help with financial matters, and nearly 70 percent of family caregivers also provide financial assistance to help cover expenses or pay for care. That's a lot to juggle, especially when you likely have your own financial goals to tend to.

The earlier you and your parents start planning for this shift in your relationship, the easier it will be for all of you to relax today, knowing you have a plan for being able to step in and provide help, if and when the need arises.

Have an adult conversation, ASAP. You may be the most accomplished 35-, 45-, or 55-year-old wife, mom, and colleague, but when it comes to your parents, I know that many of you dissolve into being a kid. You don't dare ask your parents how they are doing financially, and they sure don't volunteer the information. That is a costly silence. What I see happen all too often is that adult children find out way too late that Mom and Dad didn't have everything under control. Sometimes credit card bills, property taxes, and other bills weren't always getting paid. Then the parent gets an ominous past-due notice in the mail, at which point they turn to the kids for help in sorting it all out. Or the parents simply can't cover their living expenses on their fixed income, so the kids need to step in and fill the gaps. Or you discover they have a mountain of credit card debt.

That you will do everything you need to do goes without saying. All I want you—and your parents—to appreciate is that there are steps you can take today to make it easier for you to step in when the time comes.

And that starts with talking today. The same financial advice I gave you back in the retirement section of The Financial Empowerment Plan, is advice for your parents. Is their mortgage paid off? Can they easily handle the cost of staying in their current home? Will their retirement funds last until age 90–95?

If ever there was a No Shame/No Blame zone, this is it. Approach your parents with love and support. No recrimination. No judgment. Make it clear that you will be the rock for them, if needed, that they were for you when you were young. But the way they can help you be there for them is to open up and work together with you as a family.

If what you learn makes you nervous about their financial security, move slowly. You are starting a conversation, not laying out ultimatums. If you have ample resources that

will allow you to jump in and provide all the financial assistance they may need, that's great. But that's not likely for
many of you. I know you want to help. I know you will
help. But your parents can help as well, by working with
you to take a clear-eyed look at their financial security over
the next 25 years. Downsizing today to secure that future is
far better than finding you and them in financial straits 10
or 15 years down the line when they can no longer afford
their lifestyle.

Confirm that their must-have documents are in order.
As I explained in "Create Your Must-Have Documents" on
pages 88–90, a trust with an incapacity clause allows a caregiver to step in and handle financial affairs. A durable power
of attorney for finances is also needed, as many financial
institutions require it to give someone else access to retirement accounts. You know I think it is essential for you to
have these documents, so it should be obvious that it's even
more crucial for your parents to have this set up.

Automate their financial life. Please check that all their
retirement income payments are direct-deposited into their
checking account. I also encourage you to work with them
to set up automatic bill pay for their utilities and credit card
accounts. You can also be added to a credit card account as
an authorized user/account manager, which will make it
easy for you to help them stay on top of their account. If
your parent doesn't check email frequently or isn't into
texting, look into having your contact info added to the
account and setting up security alerts that will help you and
your parents quickly notice any suspect activity.

I realize that forging this new relationship with your
parents may not feel natural, or easy. Please keep reminding

yourself —and your parents!—that all these financial steps I am suggesting are how you can support one another. They are very much acts of love. They are the tools that will give you all the peace of mind that comes with knowing you have taken the steps necessary to help your family more easily and confidently navigate the future. That's priceless.

I know we have covered a lot of territory in The Financial Empowerment Plan. My hope is that, above all, you feel energized. You now know everything you must do to be strong, smart, and secure. Will it take a bit of time and effort? Well, of course. But it's not as bad as you thought it would be—admit it! And what an amazing payoff: shedding the fear and anxiety that keeps you from being the strong, smart, and secure woman you are destined to be.

6

THE FINANCIAL EMPOWERMENT
PLAN CHECKLIST

GETTING STARTED

• Tackle your credit card debt. You can't build a financially secure life if you have unpaid credit card bills.

I. Protect Yourself

• Build an eight-month emergency savings fund.
• Buy term life insurance if anyone depends on you or your partner.
• Create the must-have documents that will protect you and your family.

II. Spend Smart

- Borrow the least amount possible to meet your needs.
- Do not rely on lenders to tell you what you can afford. They do not understand your big picture.
- Buying a home:
    - Keep renting if you aren't sure you will stay put for at least seven years, or if you can't make at least a 10 percent down payment.
    - Consider a 15-year mortgage.
- Buying a car:
    - Spend the least amount possible. A car is a depreciating asset.
    - Do not lease.
    - Aim for a 36- or 48-month loan. Nothing longer.
    - Drive your car for as long as possible. No quick trade-ins.
- College:
    - Parents must put retirement savings ahead of paying for college.
    - Devise a college plan starting in the ninth grade: dream schools, great schools that offer good financial aid, and affordable in-state options.
    - Federal loans only. Private loans can be dangerous.
    - Children borrow first. They get the best loan terms.
    - Borrow an amount that can be paid back within 10 years.

III. Build Your Future

- Commit to saving at least 10 percent of your salary for retirement. 15 percent is even better.

- Save in a Roth 401(k) or Roth IRA if you can. You will be glad you have no tax bill in retirement.
- Get the maximum match. If you have a workplace plan and it offers a matching contribution, make sure you contribute enough to earn the maximum match.
- Stock up. For long-term goals—and retirement is the longest-term goal—owning stocks is important, as they have the best chance of inflation-beating gains.
- Don't touch your retirement accounts until you retire. No early withdrawals, unless you have a dire emergency, such as medical bills.
- Work longer. Working until age 70 will help your retirement funds last longer.
- Delay Social Security. Plan that the highest earner in your household will wait until age 70 to collect Social Security.
- Research long-term care insurance. At age 50, look into whether long-term care insurance makes sense for you.
- Retire mortgage-free.

IV. Give to Others
- Only give to others if you can truly afford to.
- Do what is right, not what is easy.
- Say no out of love, rather than yes out of fear.
- Couples must collaborate. How you share money responsibilities and decisions is a window into your relationship.
- Raise money-smart kids. They won't learn it in school. Parents must tackle the job of making sure their kids value money and understand savings and debt.
- Treat grown children living at home with respect: as adults who will pay their way.

- Do not cosign a loan if you can't afford to pay the debt yourself.
- Help your parents age gracefully. Work together as a family to make sure that their finances are in great shape and that you can step in and help if needed.

7

BONUS SECTION: INVESTING ON YOUR OWN

The territory we have already covered in The Financial Empowerment Plan includes all the essential "must-do's." Polish off every step, and you have earned membership in the club of Seriously in Control Women.

Yet I have one more topic I want to help you with; I am including it as a bonus. It is not required. And it may not be something you are ready for just yet. But for anyone who has ticked off every step of The Financial Empowerment Plan and wants to save and invest beyond her retirement accounts and emergency fund, I want to show you how easy it can be to invest on your own.

You can invest on your own, starting with less than $50. And I have news for you, consistently saving money every month—$50, $100, $200, or more—is the secret sauce to making money. You don't need to start with a big lump sum today to have what you want later on.

I think you should have a plan to make the most of a surprise bounty. Maybe your company did well this year and you earned a $1,000 bonus. Maybe you got a tax refund. Or maybe you've determined that when you get your next great raise, you're going to earmark half of your new higher pay for investing. Are you getting the hint? I want you to have a plan for how you will make that happen.

Do you have a goal in mind? Maybe you want to save for a big family vacation next year, or a down payment on a house in five years. Or maybe I've convinced you that your longevity is a real issue and you want to save beyond the max of your workplace plan or IRA. Perhaps you want to invest to help pay for the college education of a child or grandchild.

Wait, didn't I explain multiple times in this book that you aren't to save a dime for college costs until you have all your other financial must-do's taken care of? Yep.

This bears repeating. *Investing on your own is a step you take only after you have all the essential financial empowerment moves covered:* an eight-month emergency fund, term life insurance if you have dependents, must-have documents to protect you and your family, absolutely no credit card debt, and retirement accounts that are fully funded. Those all come first. If you have done all that and then have some extra money to save and invest, this bonus section is for you.

The first step is to let go of any inkling of feeling intimidated. The financial service industry makes investing seem more complicated than it is (in the hope that you will hire an advisor). The truth is, investing on your own has never been cheaper and easier, and I have absolute faith that you have everything it takes to invest on your own.

Many online brokerage firms have low investment minimums. TD Ameritrade doesn't have any required minimum, and Charles Schwab will waive its $1,000 minimum if you agree to sign up for automated periodic investments of at least $100 a month. Fidelity and Vanguard are also good options to consider, but for some accounts you may need to make an initial investment of $2,500 to $3,000. Each brokerage typically has a lineup of dozens of ETFs and mutual funds it will allow you to buy and sell without paying any commission.

I have to tell you, ETFs are absolutely fantastic when you are investing on your own. I like that ETFs own dozens of different investments; that is so much smarter than investing in a few individual stocks. Index mutual funds are also very good options, but many mutual funds require you to invest at least $1,500 to $3,000 to get started. If that's too much for you, ETFs are the way to go.

If you'd like to brush up on ETFs and index mutual funds, head back to the retirement section of the plan, where I explain how they work and the importance of sticking with low-cost ETFs and index mutual funds. My online Personal Finance course has additional information. You can take the course for free; go to SuzeU.com/activate and use the activation code MONEY.

Here's your road map for investing on your own:

DIVIDE YOUR SAVINGS GOALS INTO SHORT-TERM AND LONG-TERM BUCKETS

Short-Term: Any money you expect to spend within 5 to 10 years

Long-Term: Any money you expect to leave untouched for 10 years or more

Short-Term Goal? Focus on Safety over Returns

After hearing me out in the retirement section of The Financial Empowerment Plan, you are up to speed on the fact that I think stocks are a vital long-term investment for women. Over decades, stocks have the potential to deliver higher inflation-beating gains than bonds or cash. But as anyone who was investing during the financial crisis doesn't need to be told, stocks can also lose value—a lot of value—from time to time. That's okay when you won't need the money for decades, as over time stocks have a habit of bouncing back.

But if you want to use money within 5 or 10 years, investing in stocks is too risky. If you put $1,000 into stocks, you need to be prepared for the reality that a bear market could reduce the value—perhaps even steeply—next week or sometime in the next few years. When you are ready to use your money, there may be less there, not more, if you invest in stocks. (To be clear, if you have more than 10 years available, stocks are smart, as you have time to weather bear markets and recoup any losses so your investment can get back to making money for you. That's exactly what people who didn't panic in the financial crisis learned. From the bear-market low in 2009 through early 2018, U.S. stocks gained more than 380 percent.)

For short-term investment goals, your priority needs to be that what you save—called your principal—will always be safe. True, you won't have a chance to earn a high rate of return, but that's the right trade-off. What you want is someplace safe and sound to tuck some money away and know it will be there for you when you need it—in a few short years.

Some options:

• **Online high-yield savings accounts:** Search for these kinds of accounts to find the best deals. As long as a bank or credit union is federally insured, your money there is just as safe as money you have deposited at the brick-and-mortar bank, and the interest rate your money earns is typically higher. At the time of this writing, rates are around 1.5%–2%. Typically, the more you save, the higher the rate.

• **A short-term bond ETF or fund:** There are ETFs and funds that invest in bonds that typically mature in just a few years. The interest you will earn is usually more than you can earn with an online high-yield savings account.

Long-Term Goal? Invest in Stocks

When your goal is at least 10 years away, I want you to consider investing in stocks.

I highly recommend you stick to low-cost ETFs that aim to track an index, or to index mutual funds. I am not a big believer in owning funds run by managers who decide which stocks and bonds to buy and sell. The track record of these "active" managers is not good; most fail to consistently beat the returns of an index. I think you are better off sticking with an ETF or fund that tracks an index; many charge annual fees—called the expense ratio—of less than 0.20 percent. That's incredibly cheap. Actively managed funds often charge four or five times as much.

As I explained in the retirement section, you can build a diversified portfolio with just two or three ETFs or index mutual funds:

Portfolio 1: All Stocks

- 85 percent: in a portfolio that owns a broad mix of U.S. stocks
- 15 percent: in a portfolio that owns international stocks, including some from emerging markets

For a long-term goal, you can invest everything in stocks. But only if you pass my bear market gut check: What will you do when your portfolio declines 30 percent or more? Notice that I said *when*. Not *if*. Bear markets are a fact of life for investors. If you don't panic and just keep investing, over the long term you are going to do fine. But please don't pretend you will be calm. Or think there is some rule that says you must have the stomach to stay calm in a bear market. Stand in your truth! If you know bear market losses will make you too antsy, you need to own some bonds or cash (see portfolio 2 below).

Once you sign up for a brokerage account, find the list of no-fee ETFs (or funds) that you can buy and sell without being charged any commission. The name of the ETF should give you a pretty good idea what it invests in; another click or two and you can read a description of what it invests in. Or use the free online "screener" the brokerages offer that will help you find a broad U.S. stock ETF and an international ETF you can purchase without a fee.

Portfolio 2: Stocks and a Few Bonds (to Sleep Easier at Night)

Bonds or cash are like a life preserver during bear markets, but they also deliver only low returns. So the challenge is to find the right mix of stocks and bonds or cash that align with your comfort level. Below, I suggest 25 percent. Just a suggestion. If you want to own more, that's fine. This is all about finding a mix that you will not just stick to, but also want to keep adding more money to.

- 60 percent: in a portfolio that owns a broad mix of U.S. stocks
- 15 percent: in a portfolio that owns international stocks, including some from emerging markets
- 25 percent: in a portfolio that owns short-term treasury bonds or high-quality corporate bonds (also called investment grade), or cash

Please be careful in choosing your bond ETF or funds. As I write this in mid-2018, my recommendation is to stick with short-term bond funds; that means the fund owns bonds that, on average, mature in less than three years. With interest rates still relatively low but beginning to rise, you do not want to own intermediate-term or long-term bonds. The longer the bonds have until they mature, the more negatively they react when rates are rising—in other words, you don't want your money tied to a low rate when rates are climbing. At some point, it will be okay to invest in longer-term bonds. But for now, stick with short-term bonds.

SPECIAL INVESTING FOR COLLEGE: 529 SAVINGS PLANS

If your goal is to save for college, you should learn more about 529 savings plans. They allow anyone—regardless of income—to save big sums for college with the payoff that there are no taxes while the money is invested, and any withdrawals used for qualified education expenses will be tax-free. Beginning in 2018, money you have in a 529 plan can also be used to pay for K–12 tuition.

Many 529 plans require $50 or less to get started; some have higher minimums of $500 to $3,000.

Most states have their own 529 plan. If you invest in your state's plan, you may be able to qualify for state tax breaks on your contribution. That may be worthwhile, but I want you to understand that you can invest in any plan from any state and use it to pay for a college in any state. The only reason to use an in-state plan is if the tax break on your contribution is worth it, and the plan has low costs. Did you catch that last bit? I want you to use only a 529 plan that doesn't charge high fees and offers a lineup of mutual funds with low fees.

Three 529 plans that get high grades from fund research firm Morningstar are Bright Start College Savings (Illinois), Invest 529 (Virginia), and Vanguard 529 College

Savings Plan (Nevada). Before you invest in your state's plan, compare its cost and features to one of these plans. You can learn more about 529 plans at savingforcollege .com.

PAY ATTENTION TO TAXES

A regular account at an online brokerage (not an IRA) is called a "taxable" account. Unlike with your 401(k) or IRA, you may owe tax while your money is invested and when you sell your shares. There are a few ways to minimize your tax bill.

- **Stick with index ETFs and funds.** Actively managed funds often generate tax bills for shareholders, even while the shareholder hasn't sold any shares. That's another reason I like ETFs and index funds that track broad indexes: For as long as you are invested, there is very little chance you will be hit with a tax bill.
- **Hold on to an investment with a gain for at least one year.** When you eventually sell shares and you have made money, you will owe tax on the gain. But any investment you have owned for at least 12 months qualifies to be taxed as a long-term capital gain. Long-term capital gains rates for most of us are just 10 or 15 percent. If you sell an investment you owned for less than a year, it is deemed to be a short-term gain and is taxed at whatever your income tax rate is. For many of you, that can be much higher than 10 or 15 percent.

MAKE IT A GREAT HABIT

One of the best things about retirement plans offered at work is that your contributions are automatically deducted from your paycheck. Consistently adding money to your investment accounts is the single most important factor in having the money you want down the line. And as I explained in the retirement section, continuing to invest during a bear market is the best move you can make. Automation makes you a consistent saving and investing machine.

You can create the same smart automation you have with a workplace retirement plan with any investment account. Every discount brokerage will be thrilled if you create your own automated investing system. With some quick paperwork (online) you can link a checking account with your brokerage account and set up a scheduled transfer of money (once a week, once a month, once a quarter—it's entirely up to you) from your bank account into your investment account. It is totally free to do this.

I wish you confidence, clarity, and consistency—the bedrock skills of a great investor.

8

SAY YOUR NAME

As this book ends, we draw closer to the moment when you will go off on your own into your new world of money. I want you to see this as a celebratory moment. Take credit for who you are, what you believe in, what you have achieved, and all that you hope to achieve. I want you to celebrate who you are and broadcast it powerfully to the world, to use that amazing voice you are no longer keeping penned up in your head. To speak your truth is to lay the foundation for a better world for you and your loved ones. When we infuse our households with this new powerful energy, we elevate not just ourselves, but also our loved ones.

There's just one last lesson I have to impart before you go.

As I travel around the country speaking to women's groups, I've noticed something very telling. At some point, the organizer of the event will take a moment to thank a few women in the audience for their work or for their efforts supporting the group over the past year. What typically happens is that the organizer asks these women to stand up as their name is called, and everyone applauds. I watch these women stand . . . well, sort of stand; they rise a little way out of their seats and then sit back down so quickly that if you blinked, you'd miss the whole thing. They want to duck back out of sight as fast as possible. Stop the applause! They can't bear the thought of standing up to receive credit and appreciation for their work.

Is it humility that makes women shy away from praise when their name is spoken out loud?

I have to tell you, I wouldn't call it humility. Actually, it's more like humiliating. You insult yourself and your own efforts when you back off of your accomplishments and, therefore, your power. It is the exact opposite of what a wealthy woman would do. Ladies, we haven't come this far in the book to allow this terrible trait to persist. I am going to help you break this habit, because it's more corrosive, way more damaging to your whole self, than you are willing to believe.

WHAT'S IN A NAME?

Think about this. When I ask women to state their name, do you know what they say to me? They say, "Which name? My maiden name, my married name, or my divorced name?" When my mom got married, she became Mrs. Morris Orman. What happened to her first name, her last name? They were gone forever within a few vows. My dad never had to think about whether he would keep his birth name or change it to his wife's last name, or do a hyphenated combination of both. Men never have to think about that, but even today, it is still a question that gets put to every woman, young or old, who is about to marry—or remarry. Are you going to change your name? It's hard not to see the persistence of this tradition as an unspoken agreement in our society that a woman's name is not as important as a man's.

As for me, I never thought my name would matter. I was born Susan Lynn Orman. But to my family and friends, I was always Susie. I thought Susie was a plain name that didn't match my adventurous spirit. I wanted to be different from everyone else. I wanted to change my name, but I didn't want to hurt my mom's feelings. When I was in college, I came up with a plan to change the spelling of my name to S U Z E. I thought it was cool and different, and best of all, my mom would never know about it, because when would she ever see my name in print? Who knew? She never asked me why I changed the spelling of my name, because to her I will always just be her Susie. Don't you love that?

But time always has a way of putting things right back to where they started. Let me explain. My mother lived to age 97. For the last few years of her life, she was in an independent living facility for seniors. Whenever I went to visit her, she introduced me to everyone as her daughter and then would tell them with great pride what I did, since that is what she thought was important for her friends to know about me. Her friends would look at me and say, "And what is your name?" But when my mom introduced her friends to me, she didn't tell me what they did for a living, she simply introduced them by name. "Suze, this is Anne Travis and this is Thelma Notkin." Clearly, there comes a time in our lives when what we have or what we have done does not matter to anyone anymore. The only thing that matters is our name.

Are you thinking, *Nice story, Suze, but what does that have to do with women and money?* Why is the final chapter of this book called "Say Your Name"?

I believe that there is something incredibly powerful in the act of saying your name. I might even go as far as to say that it is the symbolic key to unlocking your powerful self. I believe that it is not until you can say your name with pride, incredible pride for who you are and all that your name represents, that you will ever be the powerful woman I want you to be. And I don't want you to wait until you are 94 years of age to do so.

NOW IS THE TIME TO SAY YOUR NAME: AN EXERCISE

What name do you want to announce to the world as yours? Your birth name, your married name? You decide, but it must be your full name, not just your first name. Next, I want you to practice something that you may never have done in your life. First, stand before a mirror. I want you to look into the mirror and, as you look at yourself, say your name. Your full name. Watch your face as you say it. Listen to your voice as you say it. I want you to be aware of your body as you say it. Go on, try this right now.

As you are doing this, I want you to take note of how you feel. Do you feel shy? Do you feel foolish? Are you finding it hard not to laugh at your image? What's your body language like? Do you want to cover your face or wrap your arms around your body to make yourself smaller? Or are you standing tall, with your head held high? Or maybe your arms are crossed defensively. Do you feel strong and powerful? Hmm, my guess is probably not.

I ask you now to recall the eight qualities of a wealthy woman. Remember the courage it takes to speak your mind. Remember that your thoughts, feelings, words, and actions should be one. Are they in harmony when you are talking about yourself? What are you thinking, what are you doing when you say your name?

Now step a few feet away from the mirror. I'm going to ask you to try this again, except this time, I want you first to imagine that you are about to walk on to a stage with 30,000 people waiting to hear what you have to say. I want you to know that everyone out there wants to hear what you have to say. They have paid good money for their seats, and you are the sole reason they are there. I'm going to ask you to look in the mirror and, with all the support and love of those 30,000 people behind you, I want you to introduce yourself to this audience with a force like you have never felt before. I'm going to ask you to tell them who you are. What is it you want them to know about you? Think about it for a few minutes, and when you are ready, say it as you are looking in the mirror.

I want you to feel your power. I want you to know

what it feels like to present yourself with confidence and clarity. I want you to appreciate how it feels just to say your name as if the whole world wanted to know who you are and what you are all about.

Please try this. Don't shy away from it. I want you to do it with all the power that resides within you. Come back to the mirror again and again until you can look yourself directly in the eye and say your name without flinching and without apology.

I want you to understand that simply saying your name is an act of power.

OWNING THE POWER TO CONTROL YOUR DESTINY

This is what I believe with all my heart and soul: Who you are will always be the foundation of what you have in this life. It is one of the goals of this book—and all my life's work—to convince you of that. Who you are is where it all begins. If you want to own the power to control your destiny, there is no other starting place. We still live in a time that presents us with obstacles to overcome simply because of our gender. But these are not insurmountable obstacles, not at all. And they cannot deter you from your course. Is it going to be easy? Well, it depends on how you look at it. You can choose to make this travel plan hard, or you can choose to take it on with all the courage and determination that a powerful woman has within her, and suddenly it's not so hard after all. To your great surprise, you may even find it easy.

Nevertheless, there are bound to be moments when life

gets difficult. At these times, as ever, I would ask you to review the eight qualities of a wealthy woman once more.

Remember to muster up your courage and silence your fear. Only when we face our fears can we begin to write new truths for our future.

Remember to keep your eye on the goal, on what you really want to accomplish, no matter what anyone says or does to deter you. Just keep moving ahead.

Remember to stay involved with your money, to nurture a healthy relationship with it, for what happens to your money affects the quality of your life and the lives of all those you love.

Remember always to do what is right rather than what is easy, and never put yourself on sale, because you deserve better than that.

Last but not least, I ask you to look everyone you meet straight in the eye and with the force and power of all the women in the world behind you, within you, and in front of you, SAY YOUR NAME.

And I am,

Suze Orman

INDEX

SUZE ORMAN has been called "a force in the world of personal finance" and a "one-woman financial advice powerhouse" by *USA Today*. A two-time Emmy Award–winning television host, the author of nine consecutive *New York Times* bestsellers, and one of the top motivational speakers in the world today, Orman is undeniably America's most recognized expert on personal finance.

The single most successful fundraiser in the history of PBS, Orman has received an unprecedented eight Gracie Awards, which recognize the nation's best radio, television, and cable programming by, for, and about women. Twice named to the *Time* 100 and ranked among the World's 100 Most Powerful Women by *Forbes,* Orman was the host of *The Suze Orman Show* on CNBC for thirteen years and a contributing editor to

O: The Oprah Magazine for sixteen. She is currently a contributing editor to *The Costco Connection* and the host of the *Women & Money* podcast.

In 2016, Orman was appointed as the official personal-finance educator for the United States Army and Army Reserve. She also serves as a special advocate for the National Domestic Violence Hotline, bringing her message of awareness and empowerment to women who have suffered financial abuse. In recognition of her revolutionary contribution to the way Americans think about personal finance, she has received an honorary Doctor of Humane Letters degree from the University of Illinois and an honorary Doctor of Commercial Science degree from Bentley University. She has also received the National Equality Award from the Human Rights Campaign.

suzeorman.com
Facebook.com/suzeorman
Twitter: @SuzeOrmanShow

ABOUT THE TYPE

This book was set in Bembo, a typeface based on an old-style Roman face that was used for Cardinal Pietro Bembo's tract *De Aetna* in 1495. Bembo was cut by Francesco Griffo (1450–1518) in the early sixteenth century for Italian Renaissance printer and publisher Aldus Manutius (1449–1515). The Lanston Monotype Company of Philadelphia brought the well-proportioned letterforms of Bembo to the United States in the 1930s.